DIGITAL

Photography
Explained

DIGITAL
Photography
Explained

Peter S Pershan
Harvard University, USA

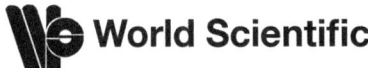
World Scientific

NEW JERSEY · LONDON · SINGAPORE · BEIJING · SHANGHAI · HONG KONG · TAIPEI · CHENNAI · TOKYO

Published by

World Scientific Publishing Co. Pte. Ltd.

5 Toh Tuck Link, Singapore 596224

USA office: 27 Warren Street, Suite 401-402, Hackensack, NJ 07601

UK office: 57 Shelton Street, Covent Garden, London WC2H 9HE

British Library Cataloguing-in-Publication Data
A catalogue record for this book is available from the British Library.

DIGITAL PHOTOGRAPHY EXPLAINED

ISBN 978-981-12-8342-0 (hardcover)
ISBN 978-981-12-8392-5 (paperback)
ISBN 978-981-12-8343-7 (ebook for institutions)
ISBN 978-981-12-8344-4 (ebook for individuals)

For any available supplementary material, please visit
https://www.worldscientific.com/worldscibooks/10.1142/13597#t=suppl

I would like to dedicate this book to my wife, Patricia, of over six decades, as a token of appreciation for her patience and encouragement in the writing of this book. For over half a century, Pat patiently endured the long nights and extended travels associated with my career as a professor at Harvard. Although she didn't say it, I am sure that she expected my time with her would not be so taken up with writing once I retired. I know that this has been a disappointment, but her encouragement is truly the feature that kept me going. I am most beholden to her for allowing me to get to this point. I thank and love her.

About the Author

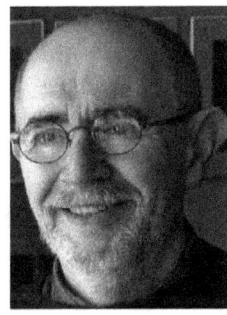 **Peter S Pershan** is the Emeritus Professor of Science within the Department of Physics at Harvard University. He received his PhD in physics at Harvard in 1960. His results on the dynamics of spin statistics, which had important significance, were incorporated in Anatoles Abragam's 1961 seminal book, *The Principles of Nuclear Magnetism*. Over a career that spanned more than half a century, Pershan published on Magnetic Resonance, Magneto Optics, Laser Light Scattering, Liquid Crystals and Synchrotron X-ray Scattering. His book, *Structure of Liquid Crystal Phases* (1988), published by World Scientific, summarizes the work on liquid crystal. The availability of synchrotron x-ray sources around 1980 prompted him to retrain for x-ray scattering. From then to retirement in 2015, he carried out synchrotron experiments on liquids such as water, superfluid Helium, liquid crystals, and liquid metals. The experiments were done at Argonne or Brookhaven National Laboratories as well as synchrotrons in Hamburg Germany and Stanford University. His book, with Mark Schlossman, *Liquid Surfaces and Interfaces: Synchrotron X-ray Methods* (2012), summarizes his work on x-ray. Following retirement in 2020, he taught a Harvard course that is a partial basis for this book.

Preface

This book is intended for those whose interest in photography encompasses both its history and the science behind it. The hope is that the book will be user-friendly to both non-technical lay readers as well as others; however, it would be difficult to provide satisfactory explanations for some topics as, for example, the relation between the curvature of a lens surface and its focal length, without the kind of math that is probably at the junior high-school level.

After a brief introduction to the historical background of photography, the book provides explanations of the fundamental aspects of the science of both analog and digital photography. Readers can skim through the historical background and move directly to the more technical material. Similarly, others might pass over sections dealing with material that they are already familiar with.

Contents

Chapter 1

History

1.1 Early History

The history of two-dimensional images seems to have begun approximately 30,000 to 50,000 years ago when cave drawings were found in various places around the world. The story continues through centuries of art and extends to the current almost insatiable demand for images. Prior to the development of photography in the mid-19th century, few people had the resources to satisfy their desire for images and it is hard for those of us living today to appreciate the enthusiasm that must have accompanied the popularization of photography, which made it possible to create personal images at modest cost.

Depending on one's personal perspective, the dawn of photography might be deemed to date to the 17th century when according to some scholars there were artists using optical devices, like the camera obscura (pinhole camera), as aides to enhance the accuracy of their drawings.[1] A very popular version of this argument, known as the Hockney–Falco thesis, is vividly displayed in the online Sony video "Tim's Vermeer." The thesis makes the case that the realism in many Renaissance paintings could not have been achieved without the aid of optical devices. On the other hand, as magnificent as this art was, it was no substitute for the popular availability of inexpensive images that became available through the photochemical processes that were developed in the early 19th century. This discovery occurred

---

[1]Image formation by a pinhole camera will be discussed in Chapter 2.

independently in France by Niepce and Daguerre and in England by Fox Talbot. The process was so astounding that in the first book containing photographically produced images published around 1844 by Henry Fox Talbot, *The Pencil of Nature*, he felt the need to insert the following: *The plates of the present work are impressed by the agency of Light alone, without any aid whatever from the artist's pencil.*

1.2 The Beginning of Film Photography

The photochemical process that dominated the photographic process between the mid-19th century and the onset of digital photography in the mid-20th century relied on the effect of light on silver halides, $Ag^{(+)}X^{(-)}$ (i.e. $X^{(-)}$ stands for chlorine, $Cl^{(-)}$, bromine $Br^{(-)}$, or iodine $I^{(-)}$). The process is initiated when light induces the electron responsible for the negative charge of the halide to be transferred to the silver, $Ag^{(+)} + e^{(-)} \rightarrow Ag$. The neutral Ag atoms then migrate to join other Ag atoms, thereby forming Ag clusters, whose sizes are proportional to the light exposure (i.e. intensity × time of exposure). The issue that Daguerre and Fox Talbot resolved differently is how to produce visible images from these Ag clusters.

Daguerre's solution was to deposit a thin coat of Ag on a highly polished copper plate which he exposed to iodine fumes in order to create the photosensitive $Ag^{(+)}I^{(-)}$ compound. After exposure to light, the silver clusters that formed the image on the plate were made visible by exposure to mercury vapor. This was followed by a chemical treatment that removed the remaining light-sensitive $Ag^{(+)}I^{(-)}$ and fixed the permanent image of Ag clusters. Those parts of the plate that were not exposed to light remained highly polished, reflecting surfaces which when viewed against a dark background appeared black. On the other hand, light scattered from the Ag clusters formed sharp visible images. These images, known as Daguerreotypes, became very popular, and by 1853, one estimate was that about three million Daguerreotypes were produced in the United States alone. One shortcoming of the process was that only one Daguerreotype could be made from each exposure.

The Fox Talbot solution, which eventually became the prototype for the method that prevailed up to the late 20th century, was to create a negative from which multiple copies could be produced. The images for the original Fox Talbot negatives were made using ordinary writing paper that had been impregnated with a coating of AgCl. Unfortunately, the images formed by contact printing from the writing paper negative were not particularly sharp. In subsequent years, photography benefited from several improvements and the principle of printing copies from an original negative dominated photography for more than a century.

In my opinion, the most important improvement in the mid-19th century was the development of the wet collodion process by Scott Archer in 1851. Archer coated a glass plate with a photosensitive collodion solution containing $AgNO_2$.[2] The negatives that were made from the exposed, developed, and dried plates resulted in very high-quality positive images that can currently be seen both online and in many museums. The major disadvantage of the wet collodion process is that the plate loses its photosensitivity as the collodion dries out, which can be only a matter of minutes. The consequence is that all of the photographers, using the wet collodion process, who were not working in a fixed studio traveled with portable horse-drawn darkrooms. These can be seen in images of famous civil war photographers, such as Mathew Brady and Timothy O'Sullivan. The next breakthrough that occurred in 1871 was the replacement of liquid collodion with solid gelatin in order to produce dry plates that could be stored without losing their photosensitivity. These plates together with the transparent nitrocellulose roll film that George Eastman produced in 1889 became the main photographic media up to the onset of the first digital cameras in the late 1990s.

There are a number of other entries that might have appeared in this very brief history, but we leave them for the interested reader to pursue for themselves. These include things such as calotype,

---

[2]Collodion is a syrupy solution of nitrocellulose in a mixture of alcohol and ether.

ambrotype, and tintype images as well as albumen, platinum, and carbon prints. In addition, the thing that we haven't touched on, but which should be of interest, is the polaroid process introduced by Edwin Land in 1947. This process and its accompanying camera made it possible to produce printed photographs in a matter of minutes. Although these images weren't very large and although there weren't negatives that would enable multiple copies, this camera filled a need that was only supplanted later by digital cameras.

1.3   The Physical Basis of Photography

It is interesting to observe that although Fox Talbot specifically attributed the agency of light as the source of the images published in his 1844 book, *The Pencil of Nature*, the nature of light was widely debated at that time. As far back as the 4th century BC, the Greek philosophers Aristotle and Democritus disagreed about whether light was wave-like (Aristotle) or particulate (Democritus).[3] This debate continued into the second millennium ($\sim$1000 AD) when the Arab or Persian philosopher Alhazen argued that light was particulate. The dispute persisted into the 17th century when Descartes asserted light was wave-like and Newton argued that light was particulate. All through the 18th and 19th centuries, the most famous scientific minds such as Huygens, Fresnel, and Maxwell were convinced that light was wave-like. On the other hand, this opinion had to be revised at the start of the 20th century when Einstein made a convincing case that light was particulate. In fact, he was eventually awarded a Nobel Prize for the explanation of the photoelectric effect in terms of the particulate nature of light. We now understand that different aspects of the photographic effects require that light actually have both wave-like and particle-like properties. Although this seems like a rather outlandish idea, it is one of the transformational concepts that is essential to the quantum theory, which is the basis of all

---

[3]The differences between wave-like and particle-like will be explained in the following.

physics since the early 20th century. In Section 1.4, we explain which features of light require wave and which require particulate interpretations.

The remainder of this book attempts to explain the science and technologies that are needed for digital photography. The goal is to do this in a way that will be both substantive yet understandable to the lay reader. We start with an explanation of the properties of waves in Section 1.4.1, followed by a description of how the focal properties of idealized thin lenses arise from the refraction of wave-like light. Although real lenses are thick, not thin, we explain in Section 2.7 of Chapter 2 how the properties of practical thick lenses can be understood in terms of the equations derived for thin lenses. It is also important to appreciate that most practical lenses are constructed by compounding a number of individual single lenses. The reason for this is that simple thin lenses all have different optical aberrations that can only be corrected with the compound lenses employed in commercial cameras. One of the most basic of these is the chromatic aberrations that arise because the optical properties of glass vary with the light's wavelength.[4] In Section 2.6 of Chapter 2, we show how this can be corrected by a simple achromatic doublet.

The second important technology that is essential for modern cameras is that of the sensor by which the optical image is recorded. Although it was not recognized at the time the photochemical processes were discovered in the early 19th century, the processes could only be explained by the particulate nature of light that Einstein later explained in 1905 in connection with the photoelectric effect. The photoelectric effect is essential for the electronic sensors of digital cameras. As we explain in Chapter 3, the sensors are composed of what are known as complementary metal oxide semiconductors, or CMOS, which were developed around 1959. The realization of these sensors was only possible because of the microprinted circuit technology that came into being at the same time. As explained in Section 3.4 of Chapter 3, the CMOS devices have the ability to store

---

[4]The optical spectrum that is commonly seen when white light is incident on a prism is another example of this effect.

an amount of electric charge proportional to the number of light particles (or photons) incident on individual small areas (i.e. pixels) on the surface. These stored electric charges form the basis of the digital image.

On the other hand, the storage of an amount of electric charge and the conversion to a proportional voltage constitute only the first in a chain of processes that are required for the final image. Digital photography demands that the value of the stored charge or voltage be converted to a binary digital number that can be processed by the "onboard computer" in the camera. The binary system relies on the fact that computer logic is based around on/off switches that represent either "0" or "1." More about binary representations of numbers will be explained in Section 8.2 of Chapter 8.

There are two principal complications in color imaging. The first is that the basic CMOS has no color sensitivity and the technology for recording color information is the first issue that needs to be explained. Once the data are recorded, there is a need to have a reliable way to specify colors such that printed or computer displays on different devices, such as cameras, computers, and printers will all display the same colors. The key to this is a system that defines the absolute value of colors numerically. To do this, one must appreciate that simply assigning a color by name, such as red, for example, doesn't account for the various shades and hues that we recognize as red. Engineers or printers in different locations must have a way to assign the same subtle variations in colors to all images. This subject will be treated in Section 4.1 of Chapter 4.

The second complication in dealing with color imaging is that the human perception of color often differs from both printed colors and the colors presented on computer displays. For example, although common knowledge assumes that perceived colors can be simply specified by the wavelength of the light reaching the eye, this isn't quite true. There are a number of effects, some of which are labeled *optical illusions* that arise from this effect. All of this will also be treated in Section 4.3 of Chapter 4; however, in the meantime, an illustration of the type of issue that relates to this can be seen on the Wikipedia page for "color constancy."

1.4 Light: Wave or Particle

1.4.1 *Light as a Wave*

In this section, we aim to explain the basic properties of waves before discussing the optical phenomena that reflect wave properties. For most people, water waves are probably most familiar. The drawing in Fig. 1.1 illustrates the amplitude A_{amp} (i.e. height) and the wavelength λ (i.e. the distance between wave crests) of a typical water wave. Assuming the wave is moving to the right with a velocity v, the height of the wave at any one position rises and falls as the wave passes. The repeat time $\tau = \lambda/v$ for the appearance of each crest is known as the wave period. For a fixed wavelength λ, the rise and fall become more frequent as the velocity increases. The frequency f of this rise and fall is just $f = 1/\tau = v/\lambda$ (or $v = f\lambda$). If τ is measured in seconds, the frequency f is measured in cycles per second. Note that if the wave is moving to the right, the direction in which the height moves up and down is perpendicular to the direction in which the wave is moving. The two issues that we need to understand for light waves are as follows: (1) What is it that is vibrating? (2) What is the evidence that supports this idea?

The physical quantity that makes up a light wave is known as an electromagnetic field. The idea behind this is somewhat subtler than that of the water wave. Although many non-experts might feel

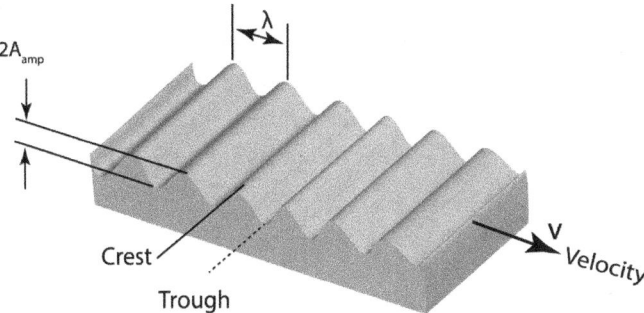

Fig. 1.1. Illustration of the amplitude (A_{amp}), wavelength (λ), and velocity (v) for a water wave. The relation between the amplitude, the wavelength, and the velocity is explained in the text.

uncomfortable about the idea of a field, as we explain, they shouldn't. For example, no one is uncomfortable with the idea that the weight of a pail of water is proportional to the amount of water in the pail. The physical basis for the weight is that the mass of the earth produces what is known as a gravitational field that attracts the mass of the pail by a force (i.e. weight) that is proportional to the mass of the water-filled pail. The weight or force of attraction to the earth of any common object (including us) with a given mass is similarly described by the mathematical equation $F = (\text{mass}) \times g$, where g is the strength of the gravitational field.[5] In a similar way, electric batteries are responsible for an electric field that will repel or attract electrons.

Ordinary matter consists of atoms and molecules that usually have equal amounts of heavy nuclei that are positively charged and electrons that are much lighter and are negatively charged. Since for most materials, the two are present in equal amounts, the electric field from the positive and negative charges cancel each other and there is no electric field surrounding most common objects. On the other hand, the charges on the electrodes of batteries are not balanced and there are electric fields E that point away from the positive end of the battery and toward the negative end. Electric charges near the end of a battery will experience a force $F = (\text{charge}) \times E$. If the two ends of the battery are connected to a bulb through a wire, this force causes the lighter charge (i.e. electrons) to move. The resultant electric current can heat the wire bulb to the point where it is hot enough to cause the customary light emission.[6]

If instead of a battery with constant charge distribution, the electric field is induced by an alternating voltage like the kind that we have in our homes, the electric fields in the devices in our homes will oscillate at the 60 cycles per second frequency of our house current. The frequency of the electric fields of the light wave that are

---

[5]To be precise, weight and mass are not technically the same thing; however, for our purposes the difference can be ignored.

[6]Another often observed effect is the magnetic field that is produced by electric currents passing through a metal wire.

generated by the electronic oscillation of the HeNe atoms in a laser pointer is much more rapid. Typically, these fields vary at a rate that is of the order of 5×10^{14} cycles per second.[7] Since the speed of light is of the order of $c = 3 \times 10^{10}$ cm/s, the wavelength of the laser light $(\lambda = c/f)$ is of the order of 0.00006 cm which is about 1/100th the diameter of a human hair. Although light waves are made up of both electric and magnetic fields, for our purposes, the magnetic fields can be ignored. Light waves can thus be understood to consist of electric waves with wavelengths that are orders of magnitude smaller than customary water waves. One other feature that is different for light from water is that the electric fields of light waves have vibrations in two directions rather than the single vibration direction for water. That is, a picture of the amplitude of a light wave would differ from the wave in Fig. 1.1 in that there could be both a vertical and a horizontal amplitude. This is responsible for the effects that are seen with polarized sunglasses. For example, the polarized sunglass will only let one of the two vibration directions pass. The issue we address now is to explain the evidence that supports the wave idea for light.

1.4.1.1 *Diffraction*

The most important phenomenon that requires wave character is the single slit diffraction example that is illustrated for a water wave in Fig. 1.2(a). The image in Fig. 1.2(a) shows the diffraction effect of a water wave striking a barrier with a small opening. The drawing in Fig. 1.2(b) shows a theoretical model of the same diffraction effect for a plane wave incident from the left on a slit with width D. The solid and dashed vertical lines represent the crests and troughs of the wave with wavelength λ. The image illustrates a wave for which

---

[7]The notation 10^N corresponds to N multiples of 10. For example, $10^3 = 10 \times 10 \times 10 = 1000$. Although large numbers like 10^{14} can be hard to fathom, the notation is a simple way to describe large numbers like the population of earth, which exceeds a billion $= 1,000,000,000 = 10^9$. If N is negative 10^N, this describes a fraction, as shown by the example, $10^{(-3)} = 1/1000 = 0.001$. Thus, the wavelength of the light from a HeNe laser is $6328 \times 10^{(-7)}$ m $= 6328/10,000,000$ m. Alternatively, using the definition of a micrometer (μm), which is equal to 10^{-6} meters, the wavelength is 0.6328 μm.

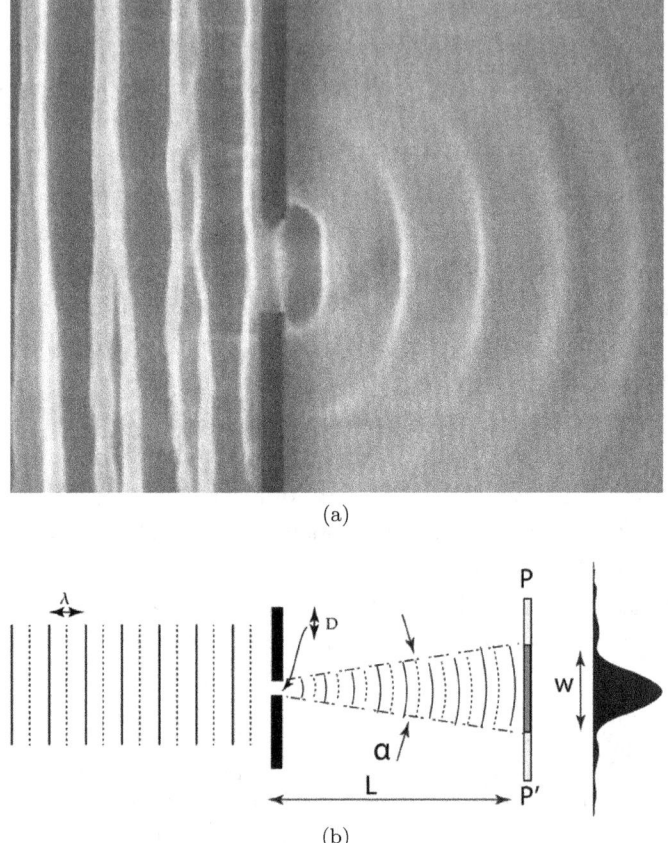

(a)

(b)

Fig. 1.2. (a) Image of single slit diffraction by a plane water wave incident from the left on a barrier with a small opening. The wave exiting the barrier spreads out the same way as that in the following sketch. (b) A sketch illustrating the details of the same effect for a plane light wave incident on a small slit. The right of the image illustrates the intensity at the back screen when the wavelength λ and the slit D are of comparable size. The solid and broken lines correspond to the peaks and minimums of the waves.

the size of the wavelength is comparable to D. If the slit width were much larger than the wavelength, the wave exiting the slit would have gone straight through and cast a shadow on the plane PP' with a width that is just about the same as D. For this situation, the wave exiting the barrier spreads out due to the diffraction effect that causes the wave to spreads out by the angle $\alpha \sim \lambda/D$ to form the intensity distribution that is illustrated to the right of the figure.[8] The width w corresponding to the distance between the first two minima on either side of the intensity peak is approximately equal to the product of the angle $\alpha = \lambda/D$ times the distance L to the screen $w \cong (2\lambda/D)L$. There is similar intensity distribution, although circular, from a plane wave incident on a round hole that more closely represents the aperture of a camera. If the diameter of the hole is D, the circular intensity distribution has a minima with a diameter $w = (2.44\lambda/D)L$. As will be explained in Section 3.3.1 of Chapter 3, there are circumstances in which this circle can define the camera resolution.

1.4.1.2 *Refraction*

The refraction of light waves that makes lens optics possible is the second most important wave effect for photography. The effect is illustrated in Fig. 1.3(a). The arrow at the left displays the propagation direction of a light wave that is incident on a flat glass surface at an angle θ to the surface normal NN'. Vibrations of electrons in the glass that are induced by the light electric field slow

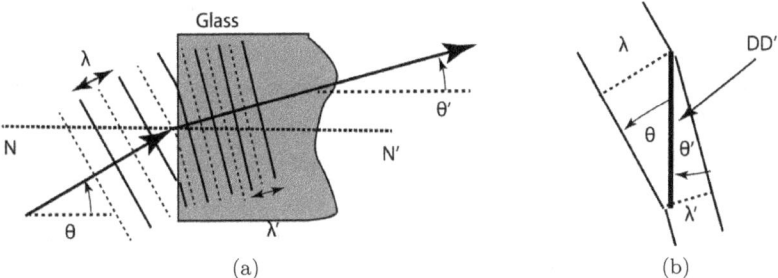

(a)   (b)

Fig. 1.3. (a) Refraction of a plane wave incident on a flat glass surface at an angle θ to the surface normal NN'. (b) Illustration of the relation between the wavelengths λ and λ' and the propagation directions in the air (θ) and in the glass (θ').

---

[8]The conventions for how angles are defined in terms of radians is discussed in Section 8.1 of Chapter 8.

the speed of the light from the speed in air, c, to the speed in the glass (c/n) where n is known as the "index of refraction" of the glass.[9] Typically, n is of the order of 1.5–1.8. Since the frequency f of the wave is the same in the glass as in air, the slower speed reduces the wavelength in the glass from λ to $\lambda' = (c/f)(1/n) = \lambda/n$. The diagram in Fig. 1.3(a) illustrates that in order for the crests and valleys of the light wave to match across the air–glass boundary, the direction of the light wave in the glass must change from the angle θ in the air to the angle θ' in the glass. The arrow on the right side of the figure shows the propagation direction of the light inside the glass. The change in angle between the propagation direction and the surface normal NN' satisfies the expression $n \sin \theta' = \sin \theta$ known as Snells Law.[10] Note that the effect of refraction is to turn the propagation direction of the wave toward the surface normal.[11] The connection between the refraction angle and the wavelength change $\lambda' = \lambda/n$ is shown more clearly in Fig. 1.3(b). For the small angles that we will deal with later in this book $n\theta' = \theta$.[12] In Chapter 2, we show how Snell's Law is used to define the optical properties of lenses.

1.4.2 *Light as Particles*

The persuasive proof that light has particulate properties was produced by the 1905 explanation of the photoelectric effect by Albert Einstein. The compelling need for the effect is the fact that light induces the emission of electrons from metallic surfaces with properties that cannot be explained by waves. The primary problem

---

[9]It is convenient to neglect the fact that the light speed in air is slightly less than the speed c in a vacuum.

[10]The right triangles in Fig. 1.3(b) are equal to $\sin \vartheta = \lambda/DD'$ and $\sin \theta' = \lambda'/DD'$ implying $\sin \theta'/\sin \theta = \lambda'/\lambda = 1/n$ or $n \sin \theta' = \sin \theta$.

[11]This will be important in the discussion of refraction at the curved interfaces of lenses.

[12]It is very convenient to treat the optics of photography for only small angles θ. If the angle is expressed in radians (i.e. 2π radians corresponds to $360°$) for the small-angle approximation that is explained in Section 8.1 of Chapter 8, the value of $\theta \approx \sin \theta \approx \tan \theta$. If θ is small enough, we can invoke the *small angle approximation* to obtain $n\theta' = \theta$.

19th century people faced when trying to attribute the photoelectric effect to light waves was to explain how a wave could cause the measured energy for the emitted electron.

To understand this issue, consider that the total energy of any wave, whether water or light, is determined by both the height, or amplitude, of the wave and its extent, or width. For example, the width of the water wave associated with a tsunami can be of the order of a mile wide. The enormous energy associated with this extended wave can tear down buildings over the entire width of the wave. On the other hand, the amount of energy that the tsunami can deliver to the destruction of a small structure that is only a few yards wide cannot be much greater than the height of the wave and size of the structure, which is only a fraction of the total energy of the wave. The point is that although the amount of energy for a very wide wave can be sizeable, the fraction of that total energy that can cause local damage is much smaller than the total energy in the wave. The same would be true for the amount of energy that a 1 mm wide light wave can supply to a single atom that is more than a million times smaller than the width of the wave. The case for the particulate nature of light is supported by experiments relating the measured energy of individual emitted electrons to only the wave frequency without any reference to either the size or the amplitude of the wave. The interpretation that earned Einstein his Noble Prize is that light consists of small particles (i.e. photons) whose individual energy is comparable to the energy of the emitted electron. The total energy of the wave arises from the sum of the energy due to a large number of individual photons.

In fact, experiments show that the energy of the photoelectron that is emitted from a metal surface is equal to the difference between the energy of a single photon, which we now know to be hc/λ, where the constant "h" is known as Planck's constant[13] and the energy by which the electron is bound to the metal. Thus, no matter how intense the light beam is, if the energy of a single photon $hc/\lambda = h\nu$, where ν is the frequency of the wave, is less than the characteristic

---

[13] $h = 6.62607015 \times 10^{-34}$ kg m^2/s.

"binding energy" of the electrons to the metal, no electrons will be emitted. An intense light wave with a large enough frequency ν would contain many photons, each of which could emit only one electron. To put this another way, an intense light beam, containing many photons, would emit many electrons.

To reiterate the point made earlier, the image formed on photographic film starts when a single photon induces a chemical process in which an electron is removed from a single negative halide atom (i.e. Cl^-, Br^-, or I^-). This electron is eventually deposited on a positive silver atom (Ag^+) to produce a neutral Ag atom. Chemical development causes the neutral Ag atoms to aggregate forming visible Ag grains. The size of these grains determines the resolution of the film.[14] The photon-induced electron transfers in the solid-state detectors of digital cameras will be discussed in Chapter 3.

1.4.3 *Wave–Particle Duality*

As time went on, this dual nature of light in which some experiments required that light be wave-like and others required it be particulate led to the concept of "wave–particle duality" that is basic to modern quantum mechanics. According to this interpretation, the intensity of the light wave, which is the energy per unit area of the beam, is the product of $h\nu$ times the number of photons per unit area.

---

[14]This would only be the resolution of the image if the grain size is larger than the diffraction effect mentioned in Section 1.4.1.

Chapter 2

The Camera Lens

Before moving on to solid-state detectors, we discuss the optical effects associated with camera lenses. These effects rely on the common recognition that so long as the apertures through which light passes are large enough, diffraction can be ignored. To be more specific, so long as the size of the apertures is large compared to the wavelength λ, light travels in a straight line. This is the feature that enables optics to be simulated using a technique known as "ray tracing," which is explained in this section.

2.1 Image Formation for Pinhole Camera

The *camera obscura*, or pinhole camera, mentioned above is the simplest example for which the "ray tracing" method, which is commonly used to analyze the focusing process of lenses, can be illustrated. The pinhole camera is schematically illustrated in Fig. 2.1 under the assumption that the diameter of the pinhole is large compared to the wavelength of the light. For large distances D_O, the small angle that the dashed line makes with the horizontal will form an image on the screen D_I at the rear of the camera at the same angle $\beta = W/D_O$ that the incident light makes. The height of the image on the screen is $V = \beta D_I = W(D_I/D_O)$. This direct image is one of the reasons that some people believed light to be particulate; however, as mentioned above, the image is only well formed if diffraction is not important. Note that here and throughout the remainder of this book, image sizes will often be expressed in terms of only the angle β.

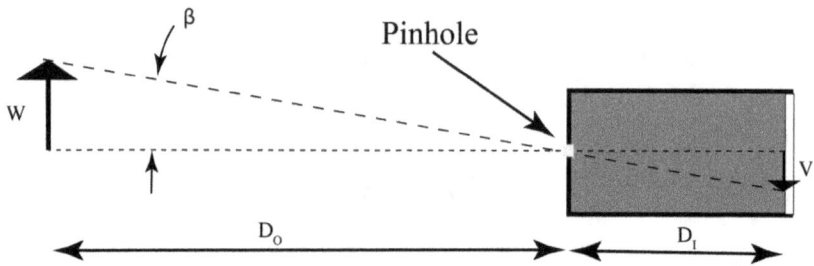

Fig. 2.1. Illustration of how a light ray from the tip of an object (of height W) at a distance D_O in front of the pinhole forms the image (of height V) at a distance D_I behind the pinhole. In the small angle approximation, as explained in Section 8.1 of Chapter 8, the height of the image V is approximately given by $V = \beta D_I = (W/D_O)D_I$.[1]

Although the images produced with a small pinhole were not very bright, they were sufficiently sharp that some Renaissance artists thought they could improve their sketches by tracing the pinhole images. Eventually, people found that the brightness could be improved by replacing the pinhole with a lens that had a larger aperture and could consequently collect more light. We show in the following that the effect of the lens, as illustrated in Fig. 2.2, is such that all the light rays emitted from a single point on the object and collected by the lens will focus on a complementary point in the image plane.[2]

All lenses have a *focal length f* from which the image distance D_I can be calculated. There are three aspects of the effect of the lens that are elaborated upon in the following. The first thing to recognize is that, as shown by the heavy dashed line and as mentioned above, once the distance D_I is determined, the ratio of image height

---

[1]Throughout this book, we draw all objects and images such that one end is located on the axis of the lens. Results such as image magnification do not depend on this, and the same results can be shown to apply however the objects are placed.

[2]The point focus is an idealization. Even with the best of lenses, the focusing is never perfect, and there is a smeared, illuminated region around the idealized point focus. We will have more to say about this when we discuss the resolution limits of digital cameras.

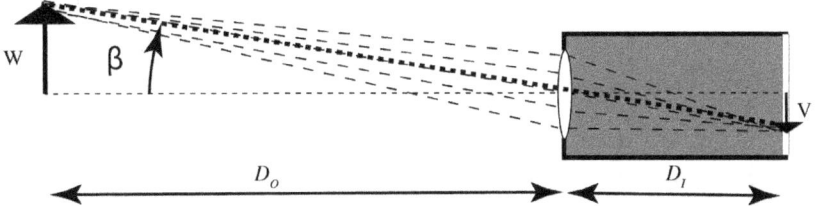

Fig. 2.2. When a lens is employed, one needs to consider the many different light rays from each point on the object. Here, only a few of these are illustrated by the dashed lines. The tip of the image can be constructed by tracing the rays emitted from the tip of an object (of height W) at various angles. The distance D_I for the image produced by a camera with a simple thin lens is obtained as follows; however, once D_I is known, the height of the image $V = \beta D_I$ is the same as for the pinhole camera.

to object height is the same βD_I as for the pinhole camera. Aside from the fact that the lens makes the image brighter, the only effect that the lens has on the size of the image is to determine the image distance. The second point, which is justified as follows, is that when D_O is much larger than the focal length f of the lens, the image distance D_I is approximately equal to the focal length. This means that when $D_O \gg f$, the height of the image is approximately βf. The third point of interest is that there is a price to be paid for the brighter image. These effects, which depend on the ratio of the aperture diameter to the focal length, called $f/\#$, will be discussed in later sections.[3]

Although for distant objects the image distances D_I are approximately equal to the focal length, the distance D_I does vary by small amounts for different object distances D_O. These small changes in the value of D_I can be sufficient to defocus the image. The details of this effect, which is referred to as the "depth of focus," δD_O, will be explained in Section 7.1.1 of Chapter 7. Only those objects within some range of distances $D_O \pm \delta D_O$ will be in sharp focus. A corollary to this is that in order to keep the image sharp when the distance

---

[3]To clarify the notation of the numerical value of the symbol $f/\#$, the value of the text $f/2$ is $1/2$, as compared to the value of $f/16$ (for example), which is $1/16$. To put this another way, larger values of $\#$ correspond to smaller apertures.

D_O changes, either the lens must move or the camera must allow the distance D_I to change. The automatic focusing mechanism in digital cameras will be described in Section 7.5.1 of Chapter 7.

2.2 Simple Model for Focal Length and Lens Curvature

This section contains a derivation of the well-known lens maker's formula

$$P = \frac{1}{f} = (n-1)\left(\frac{1}{R_1} + \frac{1}{R_2}\right), \qquad (2.1)$$

which relates the lens power P and the focal length f of an idealized thin lens to the curvature of the two glass surfaces. The other important feature of this formula is that the focal length depends on the index of refraction. As will be shown later (using Fig. 2.4), the index of refraction varies with the wavelength of light, and this causes different colors in the image to focus at different distances.[4] This effect, known as *chromatic aberration*, can only be corrected in compound lenses that are made from two different glasses, as explained in Section 2.6.

Although all the lenses that are used in real cameras are formed by one or more thick pieces of glass with differently curved surfaces, the basics of how focusing is accomplished are easiest to see for an idealized convex-plano thin lens with only one curved surface, which is illustrated in Fig. 2.3(a).

The following analysis has two features that depend on the lens being thin. First, the difference between the height z at which the ray enters the lens and the height at which it leaves on the right-hand side can be neglected. The second feature is that it doesn't matter what horizontal point on the lens is used to measure the distance between the focal points and the lens. In this analysis, the distance was defined relative to the flat surface; however, due to the thin

---

[4]This is the origin of the color spectrum that appears when white light passes through a glass prism.

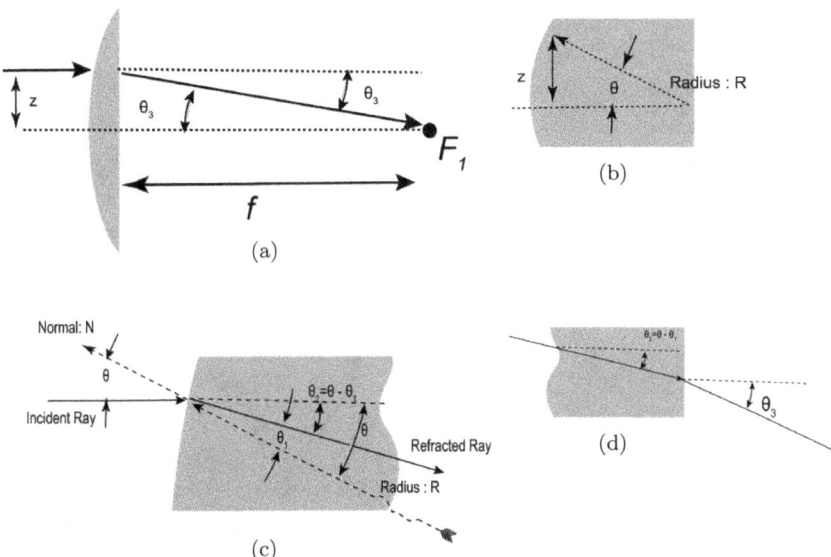

Fig. 2.3. As discussed in the text this figure is a step by step illustration of the refraction by which the focal length is formed by a convex–plano thin lens.

lens approximation, it could also have been measured from the other surface or any point between the two.

There are four factors that make this derivation simple. The first, as mentioned above, is that the lens is thin. Second, since only one of the two surfaces is curved, refraction is easier to treat. The third simplification is that we only consider what are known as paraxial light rays, for which the angles that the rays make with the lens axis are small. With this approximation, functions such as $\sin \theta$ and $\tan \theta$ can be replaced by just the angle θ. This substitution is referred to as the *small angle approximation*. Finally, we make the tacit assumption that we are only discussing refraction effects from rays that are not displaced too far from the central axis of the lenses. For rays that either make larger angles to the axis or are displaced further from the center, there are a number of aberrations that are described in detail in the Wikipedia page for "Optical Aberrations." However, these are beyond the scope of what will be treated here.

In the illustration in Fig. 2.3(a), an incident ray a distance z away from and parallel to the lens axis will be refracted at the two surfaces and leave the lens at an angle θ_3. Although the figure is not drawn as though θ_3 is small, this analysis treats it as such. The steps by which the value of θ_3 is determined to be $(n-1)(z/R)$ are illustrated with the aid of parts (b), (c), and (d) of Fig. 2.3. The angle $\theta = z/R$ in Fig. 2.3(b) is the angle determined by the length of the arc on the spherical lens surface between the point where the incident ray strikes the surface and the axis of the lens. This is the direction of the normal to the spherical surface. Using Snell's law, the refracted ray inside the glass lens θ_1 in Fig. 2.3(c) can be shown to make the angle $\theta_1 = \theta/n$ with the surface normal. The angle between the horizontal axis and this ray is thus the difference $\theta_2 = \theta - \theta_1 = (1 - 1/n)\theta$.

The simplicity of having the exit surface flat allows us to determine the angle θ_3 that the refracted ray makes between the axis and the ray leaving the flat surface as $\theta_3 = n\theta_2 = (n-1)\theta = (n-1)(z/R)$. As shown in Fig. 2.3(b), the point where this ray strikes the axis is at the point F_1, which is approximately a distance $R/(n-1)$ from the lens. The fact that the point where the ray strikes the axis does not depend on the height z means that all parallel rays strike the axis at the same point. This implies that F_1 is the focal point, and the distance from the lens to F_I is the focal length f. In fact, the analysis could have been done in reverse with parallel rays coming from the right rather than the left. The result would have been that there is another focal point F_2 at an equal distance f on the left side of the lens. The two points F_1 and F_2 are, respectively, the right and left focal points. For the convex–plano lens, the lens maker's formula in Eq. (2.1) simplifies to

$$\frac{1}{f} = \frac{(n-1)}{R}. \tag{2.2}$$

The graphs in Fig. 2.4 illustrate the manner in which the index of refraction varies with wavelength for a number of different glasses. Since these indices are all larger for the shorter-wavelength blue light than for the red light, the focal lengths (Eqs. (2.1) and (2.2)) for the blue light will be shorter than for the red. This chromatic aberration would distort color images if it were not possible to correct the effect with a compound lens made of different glasses. We illustrate how this can be done in Section 2.6.

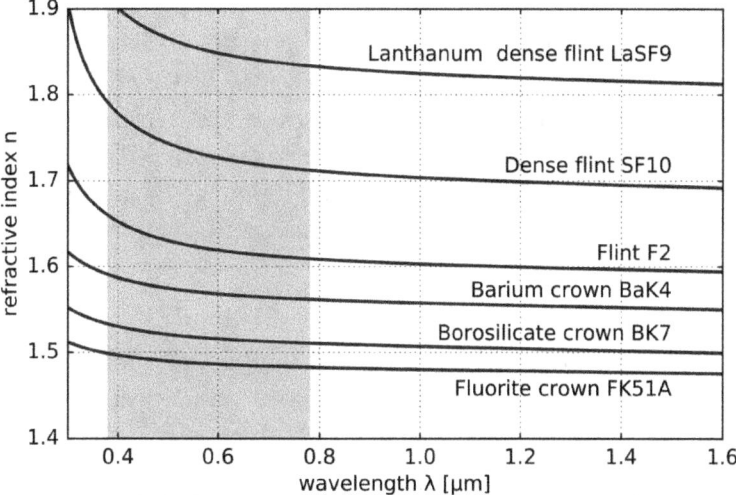

Fig. 2.4. Wavelength dependence of a variety of typical glasses.

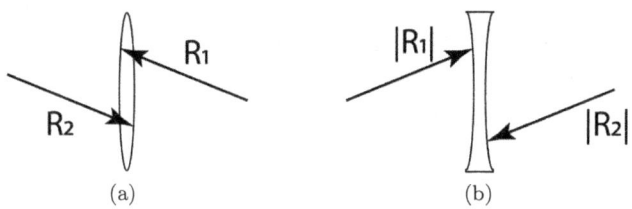

Fig. 2.5. The two types of thin lenses that are discussed in the following are the positive or convex lens (a) and the negative or concave lens (b). The radii of curvature R_1 and R_2 for the front and rear surfaces of the two lenses are shown. In view of the fact that the origins of the radii R_1 and R_2 for the negative lens are on the opposite sides of the lens from those of the positive lens, the convention assigns the radii for the negative lens to be negative, i.e. $R_{1,2} = -|R_{1,2}|$.[5]

2.3 Practical Thin Lenses

Before proceeding further, we would like to make the point that the equation for the focal length given in Eq. (2.1) applies to lenses regardless of how they are curved, as in either Fig. 2.5(a) or 2.5(b).

---

[5]For those readers who might like an explanation, the absolute value of an example negative number like -5 is equal to $+5 = |-5|$.

When the two surfaces are convex, as shown in Fig. 2.5(a), the two radii of curvature R_1 and R_2 are both positive. In contrast, for the negative concave lens shown in Fig. 2.5(b), which is thinner at the center and for which the curvature is away from the lens, the convention is that the radii are taken to be negative. This means that the focal length will also be negative. The image formation effect of a negative focal length is discussed as follows.

2.4 Ray Tracing for Thin Positive Lens

In this section, we use the ray tracing method referred to above to derive the *thin lens* equation that relates the object and focused image distances D_O and D_I for a lens of focal length f:

$$P = \frac{1}{f} = \frac{1}{D_O} + \frac{1}{D_I}. \tag{2.3}$$

For this example, which is shown in Fig. 2.6, the object distance $D_O > f$. The case when $D_O < f$ would correspond to a simple magnifying glass, which is not particularly important for cameras and will not be treated here.

The method rests on the idea that of all the rays emitted from any point on the source, there are three that are simple to analyze

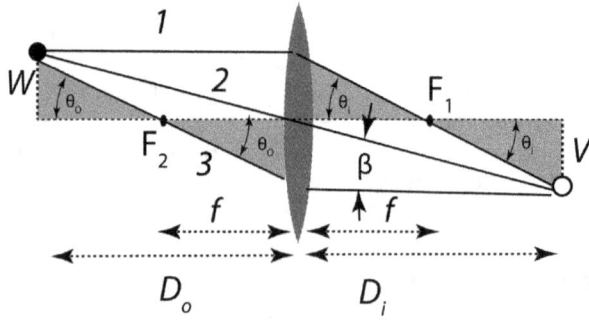

Fig. 2.6. Ray tracing diagram for a double convex, or positive, thin lens. For a thin lens, ray 2 that passes through the center of the lens makes the angle β on both sides of the lens. Reverting to the small angle approximation, the height of the object W is βD_O and the height of the image V is approximately given by βD_I. The shaded triangles are explained in the text.

and hence allow a direct graphical construction of the image location. These rays mark the focusing of all the rays from the lens, including those not shown, and they can even be used to construct the image even if they are blocked by an aperture. Note that the ones not shown focus on the same point, as the three shown in Fig. 2.6. The three rays 1, 2, and 3 impinging on the lens from the tip of an object of height W are examples of the method that can be used to construct the focus. The simplest is ray 2, which passes through the center of the lens. Since the two surfaces at the lens center are nearly parallel to each other, the ray passes through the lens in a straight line. The angle that this ray makes with the lens axis is called β. We show that this ray strikes the tip of the image at a height V. Ray 1, which leaves the tip of the object in a direction that is parallel to the lens axis, is the next simplest. As was explained in the discussion regarding Fig. 2.3, this ray is refracted to pass through the right focal point F_1 at the focal length f from the lens. We refer to the angle that this ray makes with the lens axis as θ_I. The point where the refracted ray 1 and the central ray 2 meet defines the tip of the focused image. Ray 3 passes through the left focal point at an angle that we refer to as θ_O and must necessarily be refracted to be parallel to the lens axis on the right side. The three rays all meet at a height V and distance D_I from the lens. The trigonometry by which Eqs. (2.4)–(2.6) can be derived is shown in the following paragraph, which can be skipped if preferred.

The two shaded triangles formed by θ_O and ray 3 on the left side of Fig. 2.6 satisfy

$$\tan(\theta_O) = \frac{W}{D_O - f} = \frac{V}{f} \quad \text{or} \quad \frac{W}{V} = \frac{D_O - f}{f}, \quad (2.4)$$

while the two triangles formed by θ_I and ray 1 in the shaded triangles on the right side satisfy

$$\tan(\theta_I) = \frac{V}{D_I - f} = \frac{W}{f} \quad \text{or} \quad \frac{W}{V} = \frac{f}{D_I - f}. \quad (2.5)$$

Setting the right-hand terms for W/V in Eqs. (2.4) and (2.5) equal to each other, we obtain

$$\frac{D_O - f}{f} = \frac{f}{D_I - f} \quad \Rightarrow \quad D_O D_I = f(D_O + D_I). \quad (2.6)$$

For thin lenses, Eq. (2.3) is obtained by dividing both sides of Eq. (2.6) by the product $f D_O D_I$.

For most photographic situations, the important result shown by Eq. (2.3), as mentioned above, is that when the distance between the object and the lens D_O is much larger than the focal length, the position of the image is very close to the focal point.[6] This can be shown explicitly using a little more algebra to solve for the difference

$$\delta D_I = D_i - f = f^2/(D_O - f). \tag{2.7}$$

When D_O is much larger than f the difference δ_I between D_I and f is much smaller than f. For example, for an object $D_O = 5$ m away from a typical $f = 50$ mm lens, the distance is only $\delta D_I \approx 0.5$ mm past the focal point. Aside from close-up photographs, the distance from object to lens is generally much larger than the 50 mm focal length, which is only about 2 inches.

A second notable aspect of this example is that, as was already mentioned, in the small angle approximation, the height of the image V is approximately given by the same value as was obtained for the pinhole camera in Fig. 2.1:

$$V = \beta D_I. \tag{2.8}$$

However, since $W = \beta D_O$ when D_O is much larger than f, one can also write

$$V = W(f/D_O), \tag{2.9}$$

demonstrating that the image height increases with the focal length of the lens.

This simple relation can be used to estimate the size that features on the object that are made in the photographed image. For example, the angular width β made by photographing a person's eye ($W \sim 10$ mm) when taken at a distance of $D_O = 10$ m $= 10,000$ mm from a camera is $\beta = 10^{-3}$ radians.[7] With focal length f, the height of the

---

[6]Note that we are speaking of a large but finite size of D_O in order that V is non-zero.

[7]The explanation of the meaning of radian is explained in Section 8.1 of Chapter 8.

image $V \sim 10^{-3} f$. With a 100 mm lens, this turns out to be 0.1 mm. The question for the photographer, which is addressed in Section 3.3 is whether the resolution of the sensor (film or electronic) can resolve 0.1 mm details.

The last aspect of Eq. (2.7) that needs to be emphasized is that when D_O changes, the distance δD_I between the image and the focal point also changes. Even though a change in δD_I can be small, as we see later in Section 7.1.1 of Chapter 7, this can be enough to defocus parts of the image. This raises the issue that objects at different distances might not be simultaneously focused. As was mentioned above, cameras have what is known as *depth of focus*, which describes the range of object distances δD_O that can simultaneously be in focus. We show later in the book the extent to which δD_O can be controlled by the photographer.

2.5 Magnification by a Thin Negative Lens

For photographic purposes, negative lenses are almost always used in combination with one or more positive lenses. The example discussed here is for the achromatic doublet; however, following this example the reader should be able to demonstrate for themselves that if the distance between the two lenses is increased it is possible to create a lens combination that is shorter than a single long lens with identical focal length. In both cases, the negative lens is used to modify an image that would have been created by the positive lens alone. For example, the image *VP* in Fig. 2.7 represents the image of an object that would have been produced by a positive lens (not shown) if the rays were not intercepted by the negative lens. In view of the fact that the negative lens is thicker away from the center than at the center, the horizontal ray 1 from the object (not shown) that would have struck the end of image *VP* is refracted by the negative lens so as to appear as though it passed through the leftmost focal point F_1 to the left of the lens. This focal point is to the left rather than the right, as F_1 was for the positive lens, because the focal length for the negative lens is negative $f_N = -|f_N|$. Ray 2, which passes through the center of the lens where the surfaces are approximately flat and

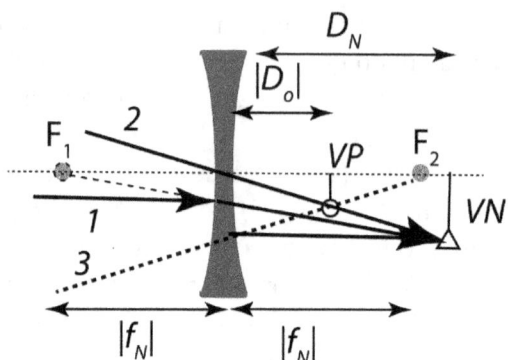

Fig. 2.7. Ray diagram illustrating how a thin negative lens will magnify the image *VP* that would have been formed by the positive lens to produce the final image *VN*. The rays are explained in the text.

parallel, follows a straight line to pass through the end of image VP and meets ray 1 at the end of the final image VN. If the lens was not there, ray 3 would have passed the tip of VP to strike the right focal point F_2. The lens refracts it to run parallel to the axis, and it joins rays 1 and 2 at the tip of the image VN.

This distance D_N between the negative lens and VN can be obtained from the thin lens formula in Eq. (2.3) by assigning a negative value to the object distance $D_O = -|D_O|$ (i.e. to the right of the lens) and $f = -|f_N|$ to obtain

$$-\frac{1}{|f_N|} = -\frac{1}{|D_O|} + \frac{1}{D_N}, \tag{2.10}$$

from which one obtains

$$D_N = \frac{|f_N||D_O|}{|f_N| - |D_O|}. \tag{2.11}$$

Since $D_N > 0$, it is to the right of both F_2 and VP. It follows that this combination magnifies the first image:

$$\frac{VN}{VP} = \frac{D_N}{D_O} = \frac{|f_N|}{|f_N| - |D_O|} > 1. \tag{2.12}$$

Note that for this, the goal of producing a real image at a positive value $D_N > 0$ requires $|f_N| > |D_O|$. Furthermore, the magnification increases as VP moves closer to the right focal point F_2. To put this another way, the magnification increases as D_O approaches the focal length $|f_N|$.

The second important feature of the negative lens is that so long as $|f_N| > |D_O|$, the magnification VN/VP decreases as the distance $(|f_N| - |D_O|)$ between the first image VP and the right focal point F_2 increases. In other words, the magnification decreases as $|f_N|$ increases. We show in the following that since this is the opposite of the behavior of a positive lens, a combination of positive and negative lenses from different glasses can form a compound lens that can be made to cancel the chromatic aberration of a single lens.

2.6 Achromatic Doublet

The way in which a combination of positive and negative lenses made from different glasses (see Fig. 2.4) can create an achromatic doublet that minimizes the chromatic aberrations (discussed in Section 2.2) can be explained in detail by referring to Fig. 2.8.

Figure 2.8(a) depicts the image VP that would be formed by the positive lens alone were the negative lens not in place. The three rays (1, 2, and 3) are the same as shown in Fig. 2.6. Although the drawing doesn't show it, the assumption for this discussion is that the distance between the original object and the lenses is much larger than the focal length f_P of the positive lens. With this assumption, the distance D_i between the lens and the image VP can be taken to be equal to the focal length f_P of the positive lens.

When the negative lens is inserted as shown in Fig. 2.8(b), the image VP from the positive lens becomes the object to be focused by the negative lens in the manner illustrated in Fig. 2.7. Since VP is on the right of the negative lens, the object distance D_{No} that replaces D_O in Eq. (2.11) is negative:

$$D_{No} = -D_i \approx -f_p. \tag{2.13}$$

If the absolute value of the negative focal length is large enough to satisfy

$$|f_N| > f_P = |D_{No}|, \tag{2.14}$$

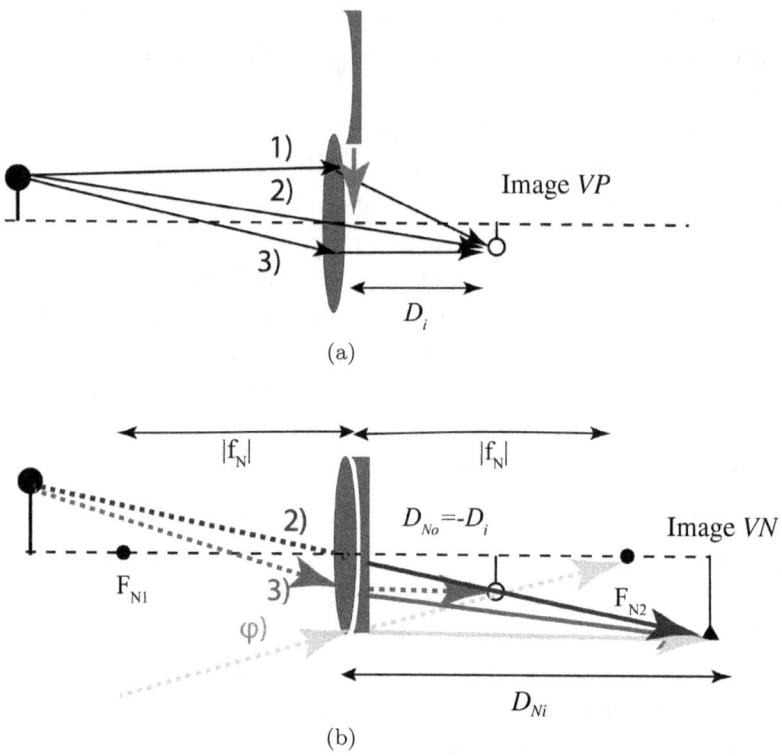

Fig. 2.8. Positions of positive/negative lenses that form an achromatic doublet: (a) Image *VP* that would be formed by a positive lens placed before the negative lens of focal length $f_N = -|f_N|$. (b) Position of the final image *VN*: The rays refracted by the negative lens are depicted by the solid lines, and the dashed lines are those that have not yet been refracted by the negative lens. The various lines and arrows are explained further in the text. This example requires that the absolute value of the focal length for the negative lens $|f_N|$ is larger than the distance between the lens pair and the image *VP*.

the distance to the final image from the lens pair, Eq. (2.11), is

$$D_{Ni} = \frac{|f_N||f_p|}{|f_N| - |f_p|} > |f_N|, \tag{2.15}$$

as shown. With the assumption that the object distance to the left of this lens pair is very large, D_{Ni} becomes approximately equal to the focal length f_D of the lens pair. So long as $|f_N| > f_P$, the doublet has a positive focal length:

$$f_D \approx \frac{|f_N|f_P}{|f_N| - f_P},$$ (2.16)

or

$$\frac{1}{f_D} = \frac{1}{f_P} - \frac{1}{|f_N|}.$$

The explanation for the ray diagram illustrating the geometric construction in Fig. 2.8(b) is as follows. Although ray 1 is basic for the formation of *VP*, it isn't really useful for the focusing by the negative lens. Ray 2 passes straight through the flat surfaces of both the positive and negative lenses, and it passes through the peak of *VP* and continues to the peak of *VN*. If ray 3 were not refracted by the positive lens, it would have continued parallel to the axis to the peak of the *VP* negative lens. The refraction directs it in a direction that is in line with the negative focal point F_{NI} of the negative lens. This is the same as what was shown in Fig. 2.7. Rays 2 and 3 come together at the peak of *VN*. The green ray denoted by φ is not necessarily a real ray. If the two lenses were larger, there would have been a ray like this coming from the tip of the original image and refracted from the positive lens in order to run through the tip of *VP* and strike the right focal point F_{N2}. On the other hand, we know that all the rays passing through these lenses focus at the same point. One can use this imaginary ray to construct the final image. A ray propagating in this way would leave the lens pair parallel to the axis and strike the tip of *VN*. All three rays meet at the peak of *VN* to form the final image. As was explained above, under the assumption that the distance between the original image and the lens pair is much larger than the focal length f_P of the positive lens, D_{Ni} can be taken to be the focal point of the lens pair.

In view of the fact that the indices of refraction, or color dispersion, shown in Fig. 2.4, of all glasses are larger for the blue light than for the red light, the focal lengths given by Eq. (2.1) for the blue light are always shorter than for red. This is the origin of the chromatic aberration of simple lenses. It is clear that if both glasses in the doublet were made of the same glass, its focal length would be proportional to $(n-1)$, and the chromatic aberration would be the same as for a simple lens. On the other hand, with a suitable choice of two different glasses along with three radii of curvature for the two lenses of the doublet, it is possible to construct a lens such that the change $\Delta|f_N|$ from red to blue for the negative lens cancels the change Δf_P in the positive lens. This results in an achromatic doublet.

2.6.1 *Thick and Compound Lenses*

At this point, the reader might well ask, why discuss thin lenses when none of the real lenses in modern cameras are thick compound lenses. For example, Fig. 2.9 shows a scale drawing of the components of a Canon EF 40 mm lens. None of the individual elements are thin. Nevertheless, we show in the following that with a suitable interpretation of what is meant by f, D_O, and D_I, the optics of rays near and making a small angle with the axis satisfy the same thin lens equation (Eq. (2.17)) that was derived for thin lenses. A second feature to note about the elements in this Canon lens is that two of the elements are negative types that are thinner on axis than off. As was mentioned above, this is required to correct for chromatic aberrations.

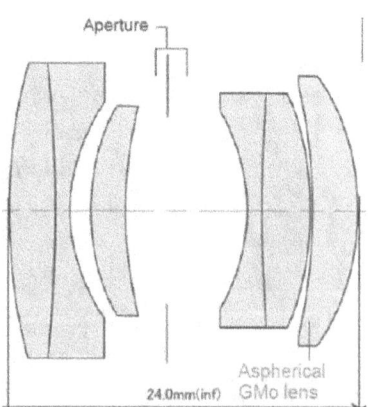

Fig. 2.9. Illustration of the optical elements of a Canon EF 40 mm lens.

In actuality, thin spherical lenses have a number of optical aberrations, which will not be discussed here but which need to be corrected for. The interested reader can search Wikipedia or elsewhere for descriptions of these; however, one example that may suffice to illustrate the type of problem is the spherical aberration sketched in Fig. 2.10. As shown, rays far from the axis focus at shorter distances than those nearer to the axis. We won't discuss how lens designers can correct this deficiency; however, with proper lens design, the problem can be minimized.

In order to illustrate the optics of thick lenses, consider the sketch in Fig. 2.11. The heavy, solid lines depict two light rays emitted from the top of the object at a height of W. Both rays are refracted as shown at the two surfaces and come together at the point at the bottom right of the image, a distance D_i from the lens and a height V below the lens axis. The most important feature that makes this different from the thin lens is that the height away from the axis at which the rays leave the second surface is different from the height at which they entered the first surface. The two thin vertical dashed lines labeled P_i and P_2 indicate the positions of what are referred to as *principal planes*.

The focusing action of this lens can be constructed by imagining that the refraction occurs at the points on the principal planes shown

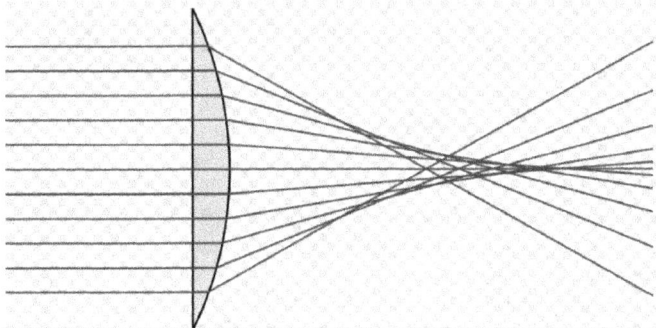

Fig. 2.10. Illustration of spherical aberrations from a thin plano–convex lens with a spherical surface. Rays far from and near the axis do not meet at the same axial point.

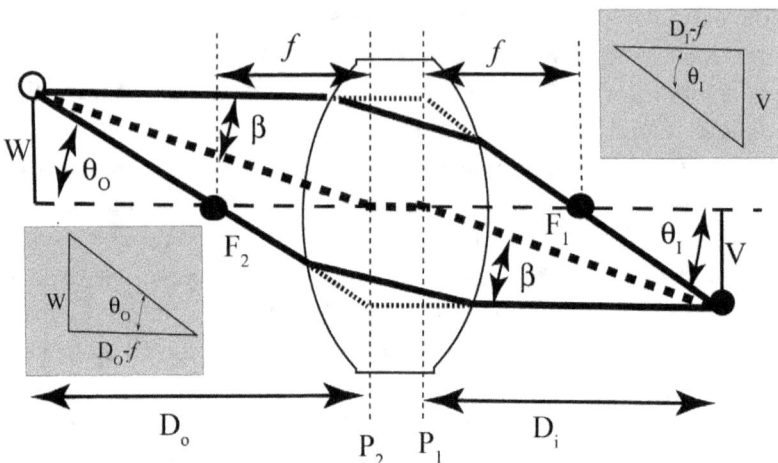

Fig. 2.11. Illustration of the ray diagram for a thick lens.

by the broken lines. In this approximation, the horizontal upper ray is imagined to be refracted at P_1 in order to pass through the right focal point F_1. The lower ray passing through the left focal point F_2 is imagined to be refracted at the point where it intersects P_2 and leaves the lens horizontally. The object and image distances D_O and D_I, as well as the focal distance f, are measured from these principal planes. The two shaded sections describe two of the four triangles corresponding to the triangles in Fig. 2.6 that were used to produce the thin lens equation (Eq. (2.3)). We leave it as an exercise for the reader to demonstrate that, with these definitions, D_O, D_I, and f also satisfy

$$P = \frac{1}{f} = \frac{1}{D_O} + \frac{1}{D_I}, \qquad (2.17)$$

where the focal length f is the distance from the principal planes to the two focal points.

Similarly, the equation analogous to Eq. (2.9) for the height of the image V can be obtained by considering the heavy dashed line that makes the angle β with the horizontal. The trajectory of this ray can be simulated by considering it as striking the principal plane P_2 at the point where P_2 meets the axis. The simulation proceeds by imagining that the ray continues horizontally along the axis until reaching the point where the principal plane P_1 crosses the axis. Following this, the simulation shows that it leaves the lens at the same angle β at which it entered from the left. It follows that in the small angle approximation, $\beta = W/D_O$, and the height of the image, $V = \beta D_I$, are given by the same equation as for the thin lens (Eq. (2.9)). As was the case for the thin lens, if $D_O \gg f$, the height of $V \approx W(D_I/D_O) = W(f/D_O)$.[8] With this understanding, the thin lens formula can be used to understand the focal properties of realistic lenses.

---

[8]Note that we are speaking of a large but finite size of D_O since, in the extreme limit of an infinitely large D_O, the image size $V = 0$.

Chapter 3

Digital Sensors to Camera Processor

3.1 Pipeline from Exposure to Processor

In contrast to film cameras, for which the image formed on the film is simply the projection of the light focused by the lens, the electronic image that is imprinted on the CMOS sensor of a digital camera must be digitally encoded before being translated into the computer language that can be read as a digital image. The processes by which this is done are commonly referred to as *image pipelines*. These pipelines involve the following three steps: (1) the conversion of incident light intensity from one point on the image to the number of electrons that are stored in one pixel of the camera's CMOS digital sensor, (2) the interpretation of the amount of stored electric charge as a binary digital number that the camera or computer can process, and (3) the translation of the created digital numbers to values that can be interpreted as the intensity and colors of the computer image.

One basic issue that needs to be taken into account in the development of these *pipelines* is that, although the idea of a *"number of elections"* would seem to suggest digital values, there are physical effects that smear out the values of the electrical charge of individual electrons. The implication of this is that the stored charge must be treated as an analog quantity.[1] Consequently, the next step following the storage of electrons is to convert the analog electric charge into a digital number. This is done using an analog-to-digital processor (ADP). More about this process is explained in Section 3.5.

We will have more to say about the CMOS sensor in Sections 3.2 and 3.3; however, one should be aware that the sensor itself is not color sensitive. The way color is recorded is to have each pixel on the sensor covered with a color filter such that the pixel only records either red, green, or blue. More will be said in Section 4 about the fact that all the colors that we see can be reproduced by combinations of the correct intensity of just red, green, and blue. On the other hand, since red, green, and blue are recorded on different pixels of the image, the CMOS sensor consists of three separate images. Consequently, in order to form the useful image, it is necessary to build into the pipeline a process called *demosaicing* such that, after transfer to the computer, each pixel in the display screen has data for all three colors. More about this will be explained in Section 4.6 of Chapter 4.

One unfortunate aspect of digital processing is that each camera manufacturer, as well as the manufacturers of computer displays and color printers, all have what we might colloquially refer to as different color "languages." A complication is that the basic RAW form of the fundamental image storage varies with camera manufacturer.[2] The implication of this is that RAW image processing software needs to be adjusted according to both the camera and/or display.

Figure 3.1 is a schematic illustration of two pipelines that list the steps from the intensities recorded in the CMOS sensor to the output files that produce the desired image. Those parts of the pipelines

---

[1]The dictionary defines "analog" as a signal or information that can be represented by a continuous physical quantity, such as the weight of a pail of water. This is contrasted with a digital signal, for which the values are all multiples of some elemental number. For example, a digital signal would take the form $V(n) = n \times \Delta v$, where $n = 0, 1, 2, 3, \ldots$ and Δv is the elemental number. On the other hand, for very large values of n, the fractional difference between $V(n+1)$ and $V(n)$ can be too small to be noticed, and it is often not practical to recognize a difference between digital and analog numbers.

[2]Digital cameras typically give the photographer the option of saving images in either an *unprocessed* RAW form that contains just the bare data in the image or other processed forms, which will be discussed in Section 3.7.

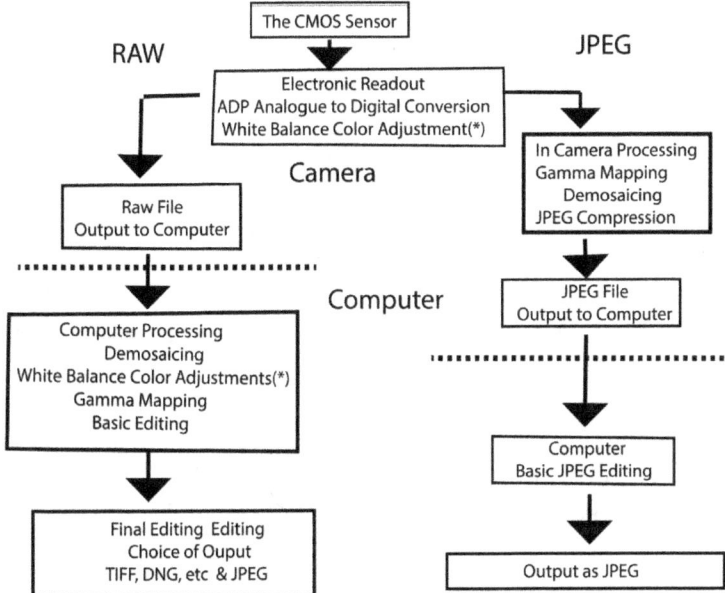

Fig. 3.1. Block diagram of the steps in the two principal *pipelines* from camera image to final image. The steps above the dotted line are done in the camera, while the steps below are done on a computer after the file has been transferred.

Note: The color corrections known as white balance in the RAW pipeline can be done on either the camera or the computer. This will be discussed in Sections 4.8 of Chapter 4 and Section 5.1 of Chapter 5.

that are done by the processor in the camera are above the dotted line, while the steps below are done on a computer after the image files have been transferred. The principal difference between these two pipelines is that data to be stored in RAW form are only minimally processed. The consequence of this is that the RAW data sent to the computer have all of the data in the original image. As discussed in the following, this leaves the user the greatest latitude in recovering aspects of the image that might otherwise be obscured in the processed form of the exposure.

On the other hand, the RAW image is not optimized for direct viewing, and in order to view the unprocessed image on the camera, all cameras that record RAW data also include JPEG processors, which will be explained later. Low-end cameras, on the other hand, only support the JPEG process. More about the differences between

JPEG, RAW, and other formats, such as the DNG and TIFF formats, that are mentioned in the last step of the RAW pipeline will be explained in Sections 3.7 and Chapter 5.

3.2 Focal Length and Size of CMOS Sensors

We confine the current discussion to the majority of consumer digital cameras that are available today. These have almost all evolved from the 35 mm Leica camera format that was designed in the 1920s by Oscar Barnack while working for the Leitz company in Germany. The starting point for his design was the choice of the same 36×24 mm frame size for the CMOS sensor as the standard 35 mm film.[3] With this choice, the next decision was to design a *normal* lens such that the image recorded on the sensor should roughly correspond to the same $\beta \sim 40°-60°$ angular range, or approximately one radian (one radian is actually $57.3°$), that is spanned by the human eye when the eye is not moved. A schematic diagram illustrating the relative size of the angle β to the size of the image V on the sensor is sketched in Fig. 3.2 under the approximation that the distance from lens to sensor is approximately equal to the focal length.[4] With $\beta \sim 1 = 2\tan^{-1}(W/2D_O)$, the ratio $W/D_O \approx 1$, and with $D_i \approx f$, the ratio V/f is also of the order of unity. The implication of this is that the focal length of a *normal* lens, which would produce an image that fills the frame of size V, can be taken to be approximately the same size as the sensor frame.[5] The convention is to take the size of V to be equal to the value of the diagonal of the sensor frame.

Having fixed the diagonal frame size of the 35 mm negative, i.e. $\sqrt[2]{36^2 + 24^2} \cong 44\,\mathrm{mm}$,[6] the condition that (V/f) is of the order of

---

[3]We will not discuss the variety of non-35 mm film cameras that were in use throughout the 20th century. The frame sizes of these films varied from the largest 70 mm film type "116" to the smallest 16 mm type "110". A website that describes these, and others, is available at https://thedarkroom.com/film-formats/.

[4]To be precise, D_i is always larger than f, but this difference is never very large, and for the current purpose, this isn't a bad approximation.

[5]Wide-angle lenses, for which the field of view is larger than that of the human eye, have shorter focal lengths. Longer telephoto lenses have narrower fields of view.

[6]The value of 44 mm is upwardly rounded from the actual 43.3 mm.

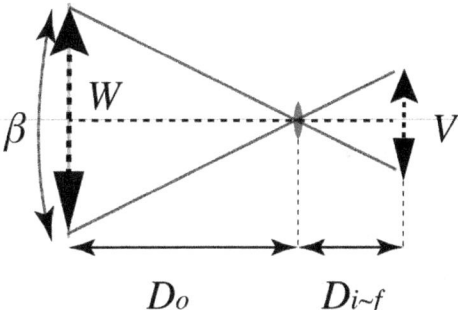

Fig. 3.2. Schematic illustration of the geometry demonstrating that the *normal focal length f* of a lens for a 35 mm camera is approximately equal to the size of the film. The approximate equality between D_i and f is only valid if $D_O \gg f$. In practice, the value of V is taken to be the $\sim$44 mm diameter of the 35 mm negative.

unity implies that the focal length for the *normal lens* for the 35 mm camera should roughly be the same 44 mm. As a practical matter, the slight difference between the 44 mm and 50 mm focal length lenses that are usually considered for the focal length of the *normal* for a camera is not important. As explained in the following, the change from film to electronic sensors freed manufacturers to build smaller cameras with both smaller sensors and *normal lenses* with shorter focal lengths.[7] Figure 3.3 displays examples of the generic sizes of a few typical sensors used in different cameras. The *full-size* sensor designation refers to sensors with the same, approximately 44–50 mm, size as mentioned above. We will not discuss the rather arbitrary names by which the smaller sensors are labeled. As will become clearer later, the principal advantages that justify the price of larger 35 mm type cameras with larger sensors have to do with the increase in their flexibility for image editing and the enhanced size for higher-quality printing, not necessarily the resolution.

A schematic illustration of the relation between the size of the full-frame sensor and the size needed for the *normal lens* with the

---

[7]Although smaller film cameras, often designated as *spy cameras* using smaller negatives such as 16 mm rather than 35 mm were available they never really replaced the 35 mm for general photography.

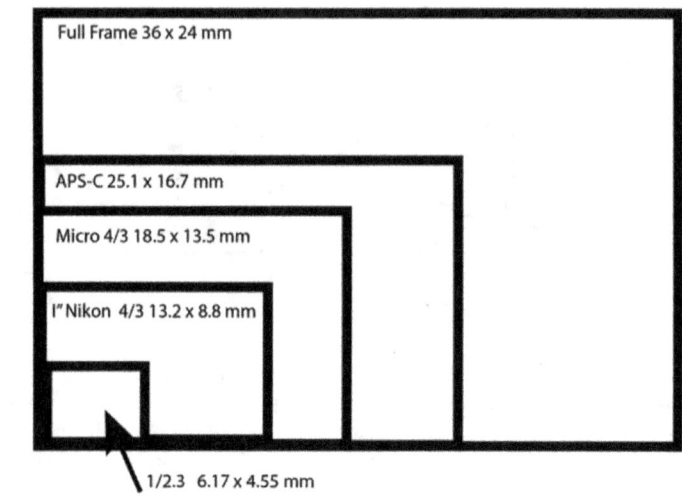

Fig. 3.3. Examples of some of the dimensions of some generic CMOS sensors used in digital cameras.

smaller CMOS sensors is demonstrated in Fig. 3.4. The double arrow on the left of both (a) and (b) schematically illustrates the height W of an object that spans the identical angular range at some arbitrary distance from the lens. As shown, the size of β fixes the size V of the image at the sensor. The drawing shows that if f_s is the focal length in (b), it must be smaller than the focal length f in (a) in order for the image in (b) to be smaller than in (a). That is, the height of the image in (a) is $\sim\beta f$ and the image height in (b) at f_s is $\sim\beta f_s$. The important point, about which more will be said in the following, is that although $f_s < f$ and the height of the image in (b) is less than the height in (a), the principal features of the two images can otherwise be identical.[8] In recognition of this, camera manufacturers made the decision to market digital cameras with smaller sensors and designated the smaller focal lengths f_s as having the *equivalent focal length* of f. To put this in another way, the focal length is equivalent in the sense that, for most purposes, the image that fills

---

[8]Later, we explain why the image resolution of the smaller sensors is not necessarily smaller than that of the full-size sensor.

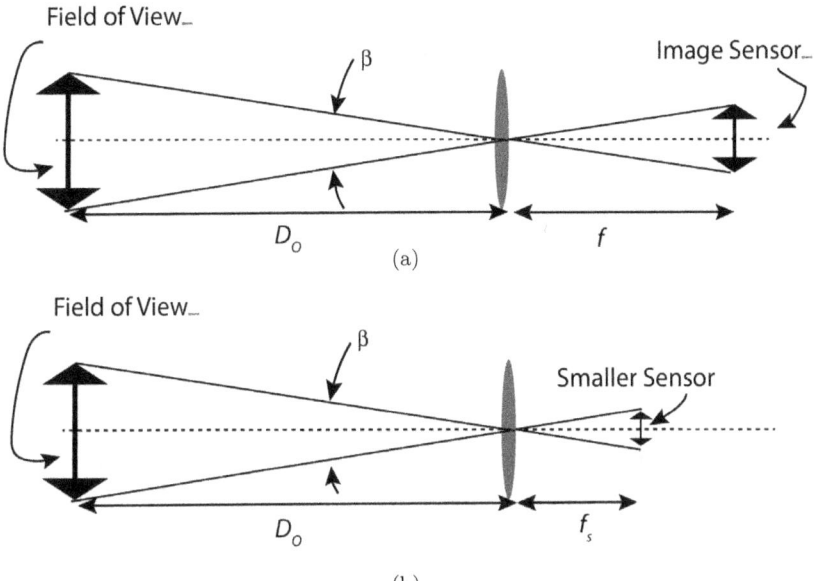

Fig. 3.4. Illustration of the connection between the focal lengths of the *normal* lenses for the full-size CMOS sensor and the focal length of the *normal lens* for a sensor half its size. The not-to-scale drawing assumes that $D_O >> f$ and f_s.

the smaller sensor is basically the same as the image that fills the 35 mm *full-frame* sensor.

The general rule is that the true focal length f_{true} for the *normal* lens to be used with a camera sensor that has a height of h and width of w, and therefore a diameter of $d_{\text{sens}} = \sqrt[2]{h^2 + w^2}$, is calculated from the marketed *equivalent focal* f_{equiv} length as

$$f_{\text{true}} = f_{\text{equiv}}(d_{\text{sens}}/44\,\text{mm}), \qquad (3.1)$$

where we are using 44 mm as the diameter of the *full-frame* sensor. A quantity defined as the *crop factor* is the ratio given as follows:

$$\text{CF} = f_{\text{equiv}}/f_{\text{true}} = 44\,\text{mm}/d_{\text{sens}}. \qquad (3.2)$$

3.3 CMOS Pixel, Resolution, and Intensity

Before proceeding, we need to make the point that the discussion of resolution in this section makes three simplifying approximations.

The first of these, which is explained in the following, is that color is neglected. The second, which is discussed in Section 7.3 of Chapter 7, is that the *antialiasing filter* that is built into nearly all consumer cameras on the market will be ignored. The effect of these two approximations is to predict resolution that is typically two to three times sharper than is realistic. Third, the effects of diffraction that are only important for very small apertures are treated in Section 3.3.1.

The array of pixels in the CMOS sensors in all digital camera sensors record both the intensity and color at one point in the scene being photographed. Typically, sensors are marketed as having a number N_{pix} of pixels (i.e. $N_{\text{width}} \times N_{\text{height}}$). Each of these pixels has one photosensitive element along with electronics that control how the CMOS sensor processes the light it receives. The electronics transmits the recorded information to the central onboard camera microcomputer. When color is considered, one typical distribution of the pixels is the *Bayer array*, which is illustrated by the small 5×5 pixel section in Fig. 3.5. Each of these pixels is usually square, with dimensions of $\Delta_{\text{width}} = \Delta_{\text{height}}$ that can vary from the order of $1\,\mu\text{m}$ for small cameras to the order of $10\,\mu\text{m}$ for larger ones. Examples of specifications for two typical CMOS sensors are listed in Table 3.2.

The values of N_{pix} typically vary from about 10 Megapixels for small compact cameras to about 50 Megapixels for larger formats. The commercial notation is to refer to the number of pixels as the resolution; however, the resolution that we are interested in is the minimum detail in the source that can be resolved in the recorded image. We refer to the size of this minimum detail as $\Delta_{\text{source-res}}$.

For simplicity, we now only discuss $\Delta_{\text{source-res}}$ for a hypothetical monochromatic sensor in which there is only one type of black-and-white pixel. The full discussion of color is deferred to Chapter 4; however, when color is included, the image for $\Delta_{\text{source-res}}$ is actually spread over the red, green, and blue pixels. Consequently, with color included, the true value of $\Delta_{\text{source-res}}$ is approximately two times larger than that of a hypothetical monochromatic sensor that is being discussed here. In addition, virtually all cameras have an *antialiasing*

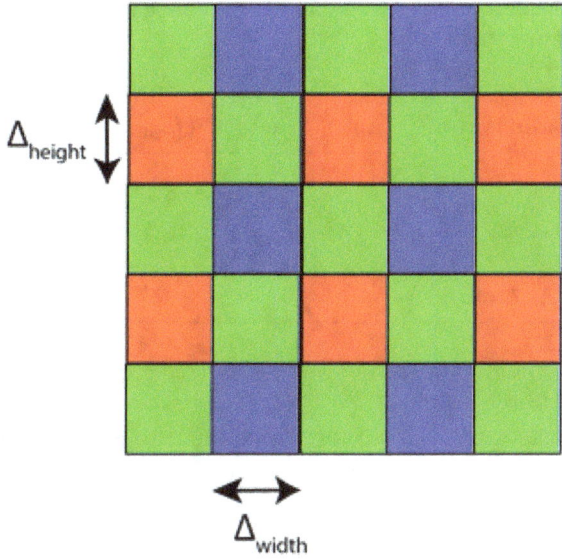

Fig. 3.5. A 5×5 section of the pixel layout for the Bayer array of a typical CMOS sensor. An explanation for the red, green, and blue colors of the various pixels will be discussed in Section 4.4 of Chapter 4. For this presentation, the pixels can be regarded as only sensitive to intensity and not color, and the text assumes a monochromatic image.

filter, which is discussed in Section 7.3 of Chapter 7. This filter smears the resolution further.

In the current simplified case, the value of $\Delta_{\text{source-res}}$ is simply related to the size of the image that would be formed on the object being photographed if the area of an individual pixel was projected back onto the object. Although it won't be to scale, the geometry of resolution can be illustrated from that in Fig. 3.2. To illustrate, take $W = \Delta_{\text{source-res}}$ and $V = \Delta_{\text{height}} = \Delta_{\text{width}}$. So long as D_O is very much larger than the focal length (i.e. $f = f_{\text{true}}$), one can see from Eq. (3.3) that $D_I \sim f_{\text{true}}$ and

$$\Delta_{\text{source-res}} \cong \beta D_O = (\Delta_{\text{height}}/f_{\text{true}})D_O. \tag{3.3}$$

Although this form, which describes the resolution in terms of the simple expression for the angle $\beta = \Delta_{\text{height}}/f_{\text{true}}$, is the most direct statement for the resolution, it isn't the most convenient since most

Table 3.1. Illustration of the crop factor and true focal lengths for the generic sensors shown in Fig. 3.3.

Sensor	$w \times h$ (mm $\times$ mm)	d_{sens}[9] (mm)	Crop Factor	f_{true} ($f_{\text{equiv}} = 50$)	f_{true} ($f_{\text{equiv}} = 100$)
Full frame	36×24	44	1.0	50	100
APS-C	25.1×16.7	30.1	1.5	34	69
Micro 4/3	18.5×13.5	22.9	1.9	26	52
1″ Nikon	13.2×8.8	15.9	2.8	18	36
1/2.3	6.17×4.55	7.7	5.7	8.7	17.4

photographers do not have the values for Δ_{height} and f_{true} at their disposal. Consequently, it is more convenient to express the resolution in terms of the area, f_{equiv}, the number of pixels in the sensor, and the area of the lens aperture, or $f/\#$.[10]

To do this, we start from $\Delta_{\text{height}} = \Delta_{\text{width}}$ and write the area of the CMOS sensor as $h \times w = (\Delta_{\text{height}})^2 N_{\text{pix}}$, so $\Delta_{\text{height}} = \sqrt{\frac{h \times w}{N_{\text{pix}}}}$. We then use $d_{\text{sens}} = \sqrt{h^2 + d^2}$ to obtain the reciprocal of Eq. (3.1) as $1/(f_{\text{true}}^2) = 1/(f_{\text{equiv}}^2)(44\,\text{mm}^2/[h^2 + w^2])$. When these are inserted into Eq. (3.3), one obtains $\Delta_{\text{source-res}}^2 = \left(\frac{h \times w}{N_{\text{pix}}}\right)\left(\frac{1}{f_{\text{equiv}}^2}\right)\left(\frac{44\,\text{mm}^2}{h^2 + w^2}\right)$ From the examples in Table 3.1, it is reasonable to approximate the ratio $w/h \approx 0.7$, from which we get $(h \times w)/(h^2 + w^2) \sim 0.5$. With these approximations, we obtain the simple form

$$\Delta_{\text{source-res}}^2 = \left(\frac{22\,\text{mm}^2}{N_{\text{pix}}f_{\text{equiv}}^2}\right) D_O^2. \tag{3.4}$$

---

[9]Note that the ratios $d_{\text{sens}}/w \sim 1.2$ and $d_{\text{sens}}/h \sim 1.8$ for all five of these sensors. Assuming this is common for all sensors, one could also express f_{true} in terms of w or h. That is, $f_{\text{equiv}}(1.2w/44\,\text{mm}) = f_{\text{equiv}}(1.8\,h/44\,\text{mm})$, and similarly for the crop factor.

[10]In view of the fact that the lens diameters for smaller cameras are smaller than the diameters of cameras with full-frame sensors, while $f_{\text{equiv}} > f_{\text{true}}$, the ratio of the lens diameter to f_{equiv} must be smaller than the ratio of lens diameter to f_{true}. The consequence of this is that $f/\#$ must be defined as the ratio of lens diameter to f_{true}.

According to this, the size of the smallest object feature that can be resolved decreases as the equivalent focal length increases (as expected); however, for the same f_{equiv}, it also decreases as the number of pixels in the sensor increases. The important feature to keep in mind is that so long as the number of pixels in the sensor is kept constant, a smaller camera with a smaller-sized sensor can have the same resolution as larger cameras.

In other words, the lesson to be drawn from Eq. (3.4) is that $\Delta_{source-res}$ is basically the same for all 35 mm type cameras with the same number of pixels and equivalent focal lengths. As was implied above, the advantage of the form of $\Delta_{source-res}$ in Eq. (3.4) for typical users is that f_{equiv} and N_{pix} are often provided in the camera specifications and easily available to the user. For example, the Canon EOS R10 sensor has 24 Megapixels, and if f_{equiv} is the standard 50 mm normal lens at a distance of 1 m (1,000 mm), the value of $\Delta_{source-res}$ for a hypothetical monochromatic sensor would be about 0.02 mm.[11]

Another benefit that can be obtained from the previous considerations is that the intensity of the light that forms an image can be simply related to $f/\#$. To understand this, consider that the total amount of light I_{pix} (i.e. the *intensity*) reaching a CMOS pixel from the resolved area in the source is proportional to the product of the resolved area $(\Delta_{source-res}{}^2)$ times the solid angle subtended by the lens aperture $(D_{lens}/D_O)^2$ multiplied by the radiance from the surface. Note that the radiance I_{rad} is the light flux per (solid angle × the unit area) emitted from $\Delta_{source-rad}$.[12] Thus, with $\Delta_{source-res}$ given by Eq. (3.3), the intensity at the source pixel is

$$I_{pix} = \left\{ \left(\frac{\Delta_{height}}{f_{true}} \right) D_O \right\}^2 \left\{ \frac{D_{lens}}{D_O} \right\}^2 I_{rad}.$$

With $(\Delta_{height})^2 = A_{pixel}$, this can be simplified to

$$I_{pix} = A_{pixel} \{ f/\# \}^2 I_{rad}. \tag{3.5}$$

---

[11]For a realistic sensor in which red, green, and blue are recorded in separate pixels, $\Delta_{source-res}$ is about two times larger.

[12]The area of a circle of diameter D_{lens} is actually $A_{lens} = (\pi/4)(D_{lens})^2 = 0.785(D_{lens})^2$; however, to simplify, we approximate the area as $A_{lens} \sim (D_{lens})^2$.

This expression exhibits the obvious feature that the amount of light striking a detector pixel scales with the area of the pixel; however, the fact that it also scales in proportion to $(f/\#)^2$ without involving f_{equiv} might not have been expected. In the following section, we introduce the *full well capacity* and the *dynamic range* of the pixel both of which increase with the area of the pixel, i.e. $A_{\text{pixel}} = \Delta_{\text{width}} \times \Delta_{\text{height}} = (\Delta_{\text{height}})^2$. Their greater size is one of the benefits accompanying larger cameras.

3.3.1 *Effect of Diffraction on Resolution*

The size of the source resolution given in Eqs. (3.3) and/or (3.5) is calculated so long as the diffraction effect introduced in Section 1.4.1.1 of Chapter 1 is neglected. The effect of diffraction is to cause light passing through a round aperture of diameter D_{aper} to spread out over an angle of $\alpha \cong 2.44\lambda/D_{\text{aper}}$. Assuming the focus is near f_{true}, the intensity distribution on the CMOS plane has a width of

$$\Delta x \cong (2.44\lambda/D_{\text{aper}})f_{\text{true}} = 2.44\lambda/(f/\#). \tag{3.6}$$

Taking $\lambda \sim 0.6\,\mu\text{m}$, the spread caused by an $f/16$ aperture is about $23\,\mu\text{m}$ (i.e. $2.44 \times 0.6\,\mu\text{m} \times 16$), which is considerably larger than the typical values of Δ_{width} for the CMOS pixels of the hypothetical monochromatic imaging discussed above. Even when color is included, this is still somewhat larger than the width of the three or four pixels in the Bayer array. The implication is that one should expect that the resolution, $\Delta_{\text{soruce-res}}$, associated with images taken at $f/16$ should be slightly coarser than the values given by Eqs. (3.3) and (3.4). The trade-off between diffraction-limited and pixel-limited images as the $f/\#$ decreases (i.e. aperture increases) varies from camera to camera. In view of the fact that Δx does not depend on the size of the camera, one should expect diffraction effects to be more apparent for smaller cameras, for which the pixel sizes, $\Delta_{\text{height}} = \Delta_{\text{width}}$, are smaller for cameras that have the same number of pixels as larger cameras.

3.4 CMOS Pixel Recording Intensity

The way that the intensity of the image is recorded can be understood by starting with the schematic cross-section diagram of the physical structure of a typical CMOS pixel element shown in Fig. 3.6. It consists of an electrically conducting metallic region that is separated from a weaker conducting semiconductor region by a thin insulating oxide layer. The semiconductor has what is known as a lower valence band that is typically filled with electrons and only conducts current when some electrons are removed. The higher-energy conduction band is nearly empty in the absence of light; however, when electrons are inserted in this band, it can also conduct. These two bands bend down to form the potential well at the metal–oxide interface. When light is absorbed by the semiconductor, some of the electrons in the valence band are promoted to the conduction band. A fraction of these electrons will fall back to the valence band; however, some of them diffuse to the potential well at the metal-oxide–semiconductor interface and are partially *trapped* there. These are the light-induced "stored" electrons that make up the intensity associated with one point on the image. When a *read voltage* is applied to the CMOS by the camera control circuits, the number of stored electrons is converted to a voltage that is processed by the camera computer.

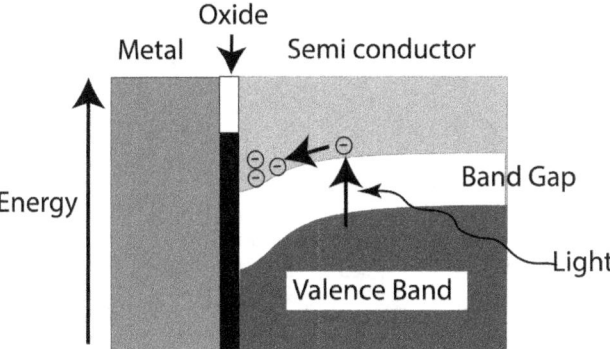

Fig. 3.6. Schematic illustration of the electronic energy properties of the CMOS sensor.

The number of electrons that accumulate in this well and the converted voltage are measures of the light intensity at that point in the image.

One critical property of each CMOS sensor, known as the *dynamic range*, is a characteristic of all physical sensors. It is the ratio of the largest exposure (or input) that can usefully be recorded to the minimum, practically utilizable exposure. The principal advantage of larger-sized sensors is that they can store more electrons. As a consequence, the larger sensors have larger dynamic ranges. The schematic sketch in Fig. 3.7 is a schematic illustration of the dynamic range. Inputs that are smaller than the value that the sensor can usefully respond to are referred to as the *threshold*. This value, which is often also referred to as the *dark signal*, is partially set by the fact that even without light, there are some electrons in the well; however, there is random noise that is intrinsic to all electronic devices, and this can also contribute to the dark signal. The minimum dark signal, N_{min}, that can be usefully processed is some function of both the threshold level and another factor known as the *read error*, which occurs when the stored electron charge in the well is converted

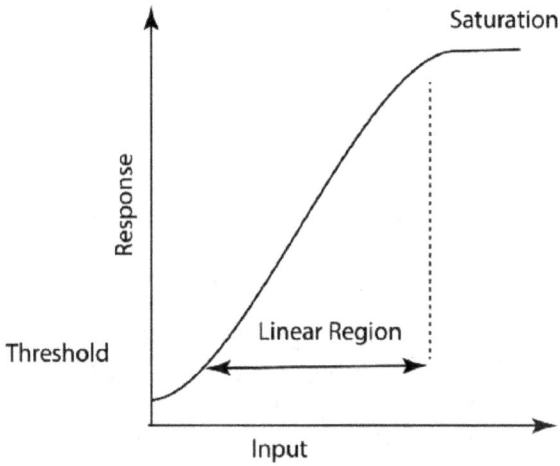

Fig. 3.7. Schematic illustration of the response of a typical sensor to physical exposure. The ratio of the input that saturates the response to the input above the threshold is known as the dynamic range.

to a voltage. Typically, the read errors amount to the equivalent of $N_{\text{Min}} \sim$ 4–5 electrons, and the practical threshold is set by some combination of the dark signal and the read error. If, for example, the threshold were dominated by only the read error, it would be the equivalent of 4–5 electrons.

On the other end, the sensor response flattens for inputs larger than a critical, or *saturation*, value. This value is determined by the largest number of electrons that can usefully be stored in the potential well of an individual pixel. This number, $N_{\text{Well Max}}$, which is known as the *full well capacity*, is of the order of 1000–2000 electrons per square micrometer of the active area of the pixel (i.e. 1000–2000 electrons/μm^2). Since the computer cannot distinguish differences between electron numbers larger than this, any differences in illumination levels larger than the saturation value are not really recognized. One estimate of the dynamic range of the sensor would be

$$\text{Dynamic Range}_{\text{CMOS}} \cong N_{\text{Well Max}}/N_{\text{Min}}, \qquad (3.7)$$

where, as mentioned above, $N_{\text{Well Max}}$ varies from $1000 \times A_{\text{pixel}}$ to $2000 \times A_{\text{pixel}}$. If $N_{\text{Min}} \sim 5$, the dynamic range would vary from $\sim(1000/5) \times A_{\text{pixel}} = 200 A_{\text{pixel}}$ to the order of $(2000/5) \times A_{\text{pixel}} = 400 A_{\text{pixel}}$, where the pixel area is measured in μm^2.

Referring to the sensors described in Table 3.2, the pixel area for the Nikon D780 is $A_{\text{pixel}} = (5.9\,\mu\text{m})^2 = 35\,\mu\text{m}^2$. Assuming the upper limit for $N_{\text{Well Max}} = 2000 \times 35 = 70,000$ electrons, the dynamic range of the sensor for the Nikon D780 would be about $70,000/5 = 14,000$, which is considerably larger than the dynamic range of about 1,000 for the human eye when it is not allowed enough time to adapt.

Table 3.2. Examples of the specifications for one specific full-frame CMOS sensor and another very small one. The pixel numbers of the CMOS sensor is given by the product $N_{\text{width}} \times N_{\text{height}} = N_{\text{pix}}$.

Sensor	w mm	N_{width} pixels	h mm	N_{height} pixels	N_{pix} Megapixels	$\Delta_{\text{height}} = \Delta_{\text{width}}$ μm
Nikon D780	35.9	6048	23.9	4024	25	5.9
Nikon Coolpix W150	4.7	4160	3.5	3120	13	1.1

It is also larger than the range of 258 that is typical of computer displays.[13] For smaller cameras, such as the Coolpix W150 with a 1/3.1 sensor, the pixel dimensions are only $\Delta_{\text{height}} \sim 1.1 \, \mu$m and $N_{\text{Well Max}} = 2400$, with a dynamic range of slightly less than 500. The principal advantage of the larger dynamic range of more expensive cameras is the greater scope that photo editors have for recovering information that would otherwise be lost in the darker and brighter ranges of the image.

3.5 ADU or Analog-to-Digital Conversion

The next step in the pipeline is the conversion of the electrical charge stored in the CMOS well to digital numbers that the computer can process. There are two numbers that the conversion process depends on. The first is the *system gain* (SG), which controls the digital numbers that are produced by a given number of electrons in the well. The digital numbers from this conversion are referred to as *analog-to-digital units* (ADU). The system gain is defined as the ratio

$$SG = N_{\text{electrons}}/\text{ADU}. \qquad (3.8)$$

One obvious advantage of smaller SG is that when reduced brightness causes the number of electrons to be reduced, a smaller SG will produce the same ADU as a brighter exposure. Unfortunately, smaller numbers of electrons are accompanied by statistical errors that cause something called *image speckling*, which is illustrated in Fig. 7.5 at the end of Chapter 7.

Although the operator can vary the SG, in most cameras, the common standard base is about 25. Thus, for a full-frame sensor, such as that described in Section 3.2, for which the maximum number of electrons that can be stored in a single pixel without saturation is of the order of 70,000, the maximum ADU $\sim 70{,}000/25 = 2{,}800$. This then is typically the largest ADU that would seem to be required for the signal recorded in the computer with this sensor. The notation commonly used is to express this as a power $2^{(11.45)}$, which is slightly

---

[13]With adaptation, human vision has a much larger dynamic range.

less than $2^{12} = 4096$. It is noteworthy that the numbers defined this way are smaller than the value of $2^{12} = (4{,}096)$, $2^{14} = (16{,}383)$, or $2^{16} = (65{,}535)$, that correspond to the values of 12, 14, or 16 that are typically quoted as the *bit depth* of consumer cameras. Since the *bit depth* refers to the digital capacity of the camera processor, it is clear that the cameras have excess capacity that can be used for various aspects of image processing. On the other hand, the reader should be aware that virtually all computer displays are limited to a range of $2^8 = 256$ values for each of red, green, and blue.[14] Thus, however large the dynamic range of the sensor or editor, the final image to be displayed or printed must be reduced to no more than the practical 256 values of the final displays.

3.6 Camera to Computer, Gamma Mapping

A standard complication in the pipelines for all digital cameras is what is known as the nonlinear gamma (γ)-mapping process. The numbers recorded from each pixel of a CMOS sensor are a measure of the light intensity incident on that pixel. These recorded numbers, which are linearly proportional to the incident intensity, are assigned values that vary incrementally from zero with no light through integer values up to a maximum that is set by the ADU processor.[15] The γ-mapping process translates these numerical values to a different numerical scale that bears a resemblance to the way our eyes perceive brightness rather than incident intensity. Although this seems like a natural thing to do, as will be explained in the following, it is not the prime reason for doing it. The belief that γ-mapping is motived by our vision is a common misconception.[16]

---

[14]Note that if one starts the count of values from $0, 1, 2, 3, \ldots$, the largest number possible for 8 bits is $2^8 - 1$, or 255. For example, 3 bits, or $2^3 = 8$ values, only run to a maximum of $7 = 2^8 - 1$, i.e. 0, 1, 2, 3, 4, 5, 6, 7.

[15]This is typically the bit depth of the processor.

[16]One site that explains this in detail is https://www.eizo.com/library/basics/lcd_display_gamma/. As weill be explained below the initial γ-mapping of the data received from the camera, which is done for technical reasons, is eventually reversed in order that the displayed colors are correct.

Before proceeding further, it is useful to understand the basics of human visual perception. Our vision is governed by a certain principle known as either Weber's or Fechner's law. Weber's law states that under normal levels, an increase in ΔI in the intensity of light in the presence of a background light intensity I induces an increase in human perception ΔP that is smaller when the intensity is brighter. A mathematical expression for Weber's law is

$$\Delta P = K_w \Delta I / I, \tag{3.9}$$

which is also known as the *Weber fraction*. One can show mathematically that this is equivalent to Fechner's law, which states that the perceived level P is given by

$$P = K_w \ln(I/I_O), \tag{3.10}$$

where I_O is an adjustable constant.

One problem with this expression is that it cannot really be used for small values of I, i.e. when $I/I_O \to 0$, since that would lead to negative values of P. A practical approximation to Fechner's law that doesn't have this problem is the γ-form

$$P_\gamma = (I/I_O)^{1/\gamma}, \tag{3.11}$$

where $\gamma \approx 2$.[17] The sketch in Fig. 3.8 shows both the γ-form and Fechner's law with intensity I normalized to a maximum value of unity. For most of the intensity range, they are qualitatively similar; however, as was just said, for small values of I, the response predicted by Fechner's law falls to unphysically small values. For most purposes, the γ-form is taken to be a better representation of the visual response; however, as said above, this is not the prime reason for γ-mapping. The most important property of both these forms, which is clearly seen in Eq. (3.9), is the fact that at small intensities, the change in ΔP produced by a small incremental change in ΔI becomes larger than for larger intensities. The γ-mapping process transforms the data sent to the computer into a form that better corresponds to this aspect of human perception; however, as

---

[17]The value actually mostly used is $\gamma = 2.2$.

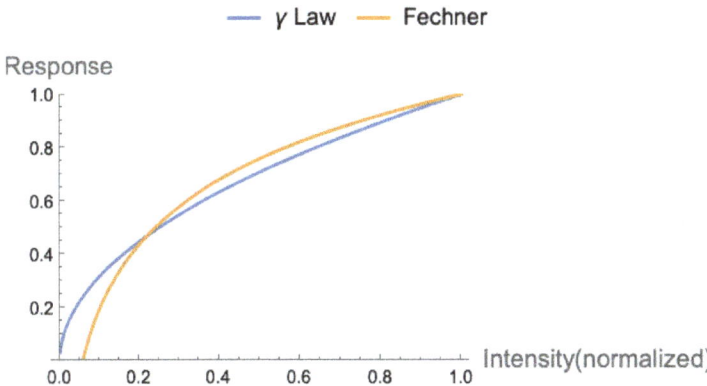

Fig. 3.8. Illustration comparing the γ-form and Fecnher's law. The data have been normalized to the maximum value of unit intensity.

was said above, this is not the real reason for the γ-mapping. This is explained in the following.

To be specific, the way γ-mapping is done in the processors is that the intensity data are first normalized by dividing them by the largest available digital value in the processor. This produces values of x, which range from 0 to 1. The γ-mapping converts these to a variable $y = x^{1/\gamma}$, where γ is approximately 2.[18] The values of y also range from 0 to 1. An expansion of this mapping for low values of x is shown schematically in Fig. 3.9, along with Table 3.3, which displays the first five values.[19]

One problem with the recorded data that can be seen here is that although the allowed values of x are evenly spaced, the values for y are not. In the dark portion of an image (i.e. small x), the allowed values for y are spaced such that for a given range of Δx, the range of Δy needed for these points is larger than the range of Δx. In this illustrative example, between $y = 0$ and 0.2, there are only two or three values of x compared to about a dozen values for the same range of Δy at larger x. To see this another way, if Eq. (3.11) is

---

[18]As mentioned above, the value is actually more like 2.2.

[19]The graph is schematic since the number of points in the real mapping is either $2^8 - 256$ or larger, and the steps in x are $\sim 1/256 = 0.004$ or smaller.

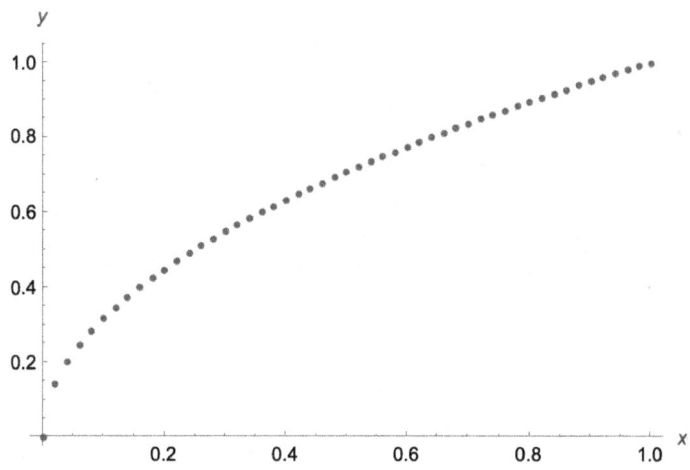

Fig. 3.9. Schematic illustration of γ-mapping of the x values to y.

Table 3.3. Numerical values of the first five rows for the data in Fig. 3.9.

x	y
0.00	0.000
0.01	0.100
0.02	0.141
0.03	0.173
0.04	0.200

expressed as $y = x^{1/\gamma}$, one can show that the incremental changes Δx and Δy are related by

$$\Delta y = \frac{\Delta x}{2x^{1/2}}. \tag{3.12}$$

This is an explicit demonstration of what was said above: The incremental changes in Δx for small x induce larger changes in Δy than for larger x. Although we do not discuss it here, one of the benefits of γ-mapping is that the various editing procedures for extracting features that are not visible in either the dark underexposed or bright overexposed portions of the images are better managed if the data are processed in the γ-mapped y form. In other words, the γ-mapped data can be treated more efficiently than the original x form.

The second reason for γ-mapping is that the physical process by which the data are displayed by the electronics actually follows an x^γ transformation that inverts the γ-mapping. To help understand this, the sketch in Fig. 3.10(a) illustrates the three forms of the data. The line (x) shows the original data that are linear in x, $(x^{1/\gamma})$ shows the γ-mapping, and (x^γ) shows a transformation that would reverse the γ-mapping. The key point about this last form is that essentially all computer displays have the property that the displayed data are in the x^γ form. For example, Fig. 3.10(b) shows how the image data are sent to the display on a Macintosh computer. As was just said, this form is ubiquitous on all computer displays. The γ transformation is needed to put the data stored in the computer in a form such that, when displayed on the monitor, the intensity levels are proportional to the illuminated intensity. In other words, were it not for γ-mapping, the data sent to the display would have been proportional to x^γ rather than to the original x-form of the original image. This is really the principal reason for γ-mapping.

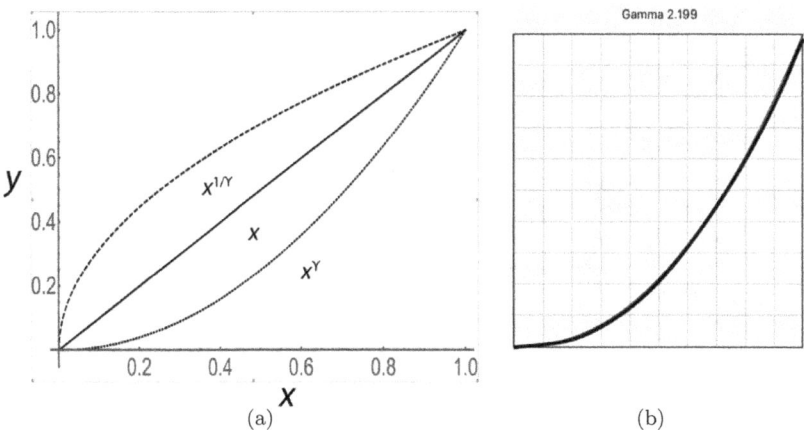

Fig. 3.10. (a) Curves for $x^{1/\gamma}$, x, and x^γ demonstrating the γ-mapping, as discussed in the text. (b) Copy of the monitor response curve from a MacIntosh computer that demonstrates the way in which liquid crystal monitors reverse the γ-mapping to produce the final image.

3.7 Output File Choices

This is the point where a choice must be made between the two pipelines shown in Fig. 3.1. As mentioned above, high-end cameras employ both pipelines and save images in both a RAW form, which contains all the recorded image data with absolutely no processing and a smaller processed JPEG form, in which some data have been discarded. More about the differences between these two file types will be discussed in Chapter 5; however, for now, the reader should appreciate that professionals and those seeking more sophistication prefer the RAW form because it stores all of the information in the original image and consequently maximizes the image editing flexibility. Unfortunately, not only are the RAW files that are sent to a computer labeled differently by each camera manufacturer (i.e. CR2, NEF, ARW, etc., by Canon, Nikon, Sony, etc.) but the data formats and the computer codes for reading them are also different. In contrast, JPEG processing allows images to be read on both the camera and virtually all computers.[20]

Depending on the amount of data that is discarded in the selected JPEG process (i.e. high or low quality), the JPEG files are typically ~2–20 times smaller than the unprocessed RAW files. See Table 3.4 for examples. For most purposes, the effect of the JPEG discarding is not noticeable; however, JPEG files do not contain some image details that could have been recovered in the editing of RAW files.

Table 3.4. Examples of the typical sizes for the same image saved in both RAW and JPEG forms. The image is from a camera with a 13.2 mm × 8.8 mm CMOS sensor that has approximately 20 Megapixels.

File format	File size (MB = Megabytes)
RAW	21.4 MB
High-quality JPEG	15.2 MB
Low-quality JPEG	1.0 MB

---

[20]JPEG files can be saved in either high, low, or intermediate quality. This will be elaborated upon in Section 5.3 of Chapter 5.

We will return in Chapter 5 to discuss the processing that is done to produce the final images from the RAW data; however, in view of the fact that accurate color rendition forms the principal feature of these processes, we discuss color before returning to elaborate on the processed files. The TIFF and DNG file types mentioned in Fig. 3.1 are discussed in the following. Either one of these can be used to edit the RAW data.

Chapter 4

Color

The principal issue in recording, printing, and computer display of color images is the requirement for a quantitative method to specify color such that technicians in different locations around the globe will be able to communicate the information needed to exactly reproduce image colors. The method established in 1931 by the Commission Internationale d'Eclairage (CIE, 1931) for doing that is described in the following section. The complication already mentioned is that human vision does not perceive colors in the same way that color is recorded by a digital camera. Thus, there is a need for a procedure to translate the CIE-coded color information recorded in the camera into a form that is consistent with the colors perceived by the eye. This is discussed later in the chapter.

4.1 Quantitative Color Definition

The classic color matching experiment designed by the CIE (1931) is illustrated in Fig. 4.1. Light from three lamps emitting the CIE color primary wavelengths of blue ($\lambda = 436$ nm), green ($\lambda = 546$ nm), and red ($\lambda = 700$ nm) is directed to overlap on a white screen. Light from a fourth test lamp with an adjustable wavelength illuminates an adjacent white screen. In the experiment, the intensities of the three primaries are adjusted until the perceived color in the region of overlap between the three primary lights matches the color of the test lamp. The process continues as the wavelength of the test lamp varies over the range of colors that the human eye can see.

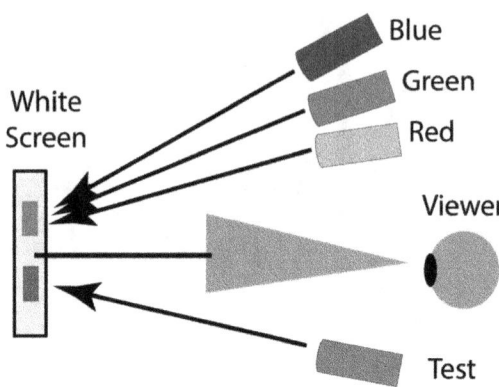

Fig. 4.1. Schematic illustration of the classic color matching experiment.

The results of the matching intensities of the blue, green, and red primaries for each wavelength of the test lamp are shown as the color matching curves $b(\lambda)$, $g(\lambda)$, and $r(\lambda)$, respectively, in the top part of Fig. 4.2.[1]

One inconvenient feature of these curves is that to match the test color in the region between 450 and 550 nm, it proved necessary to add to the test color some of the primary red light. This is the reason why the red matching function is negative between 450 and 550 nm. Fortunately, the CIE was able to devise a mathematical method to produce the $\bar{x}(\lambda)$, $\bar{y}(\lambda)$, and $\bar{z}(\lambda)$ matching curves shown in the lower part of Fig. 4.2 that have been constructed to be positive for all wavelengths. The three matching functions, $\bar{x}(\lambda), \bar{y}(\lambda)$, and $\bar{z}(\lambda)$ are normalized such that the area under all three are equal. The process that establishes the equal areas makes use of the mathematical process known as integration, which is expressed in Eq. (4.1):

$$\int \bar{x}(\lambda)d\lambda = \int \bar{y}(\lambda)d\lambda = \int \bar{z}(\lambda)d\lambda. \qquad (4.1)$$

---

[1]This is an example of the phenomenon referred to as *metamerism*, in which the same perceived colors can be produced with light composed of different wavelengths.

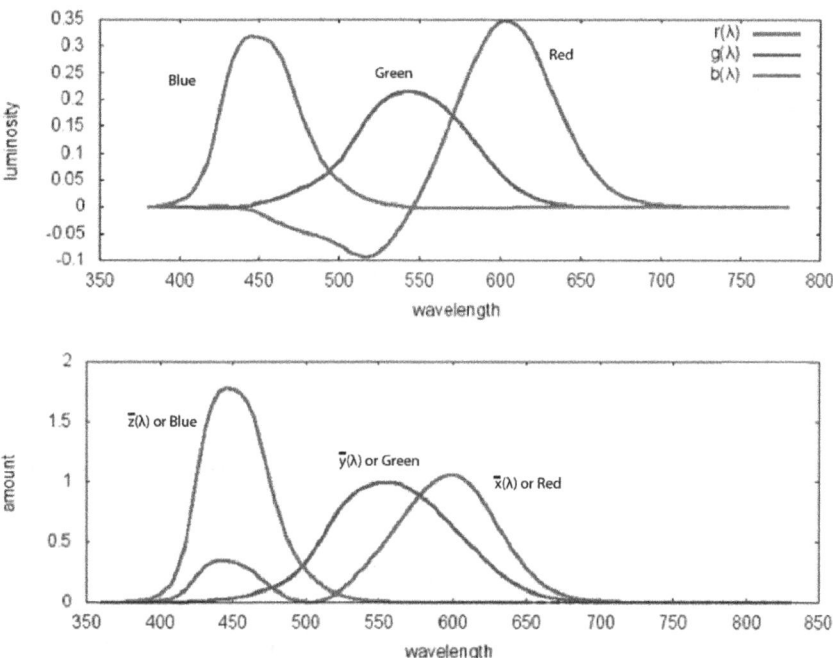

Fig. 4.2. Color matching functions: The upper figure displays the simple matching functions obtained using the CIE-defined primaries. The lower panel displays the revised matching functions that have been adjusted to eliminate the negative values between 450 and 550 nm in the upper panel. These three curves are created such that the areas under them are all equal to unity. Mathematically, the values of the integrals given by Eq. (4.1) are equal to one.

These integral expressions are the mathematical way to calculate the area under the curves in both the lower portions of Figs. 4.2 and 4.4.

The three matching functions, $\bar{x}(\lambda), \bar{y}(\lambda)$, and $\bar{z}(\lambda)$, can now be employed to calculate the three numbers, X, Y, and Z, called *tristimulus values*, that define the colors. These numbers form what is known as the CIE XYZ color space in the same way that conventional three-position coordinates define a point in a 3D geometric space. To put this another way, the triplet of XYZ values defines a color that can be universally reproduced. These are the numbers that are recorded in the digital camera processor. More about color spaces is discussed in Section 4.4.

As illustrated in the following, the values of the tristimulus XYZ triplets for light with any spectral distribution $S(\lambda)$ are obtained by integration of the product of $S(\lambda)$ with the relevant $\bar{x}(\lambda), \bar{y}(\lambda)$, and $\bar{z}(\lambda)$ matching functions, as given by

$$X = \int S(\lambda)\bar{x}(\lambda)d\lambda \quad Y = \int S(\lambda)\bar{y}(\lambda)d\lambda \quad Z = \int S(\lambda)\bar{z}(\lambda)d\lambda.$$

(4.2)

In the example of a test lamp whose spectral distribution is a sharp spike at a single wavelength of 450 nm the results for X, Y, Z are illustrated in Fig. 4.3(a). The three small circles that mark the intersection between the spike at $\lambda = 450$ nm and the red, green, and blue response curves indicate the values $X = \bar{x}(450) = 0.336, Y = \bar{y}(450) = 0.038$, and $Z = \bar{z}(450) = 1.772$. Similarly, the tristimulus values for $\lambda = 600$ nm that are illustrated in Fig. 4.3(b) are $X = \bar{x}(600) = 1.062, Y = \bar{y}(600) = 0.631$, and $Z = \bar{z}(600) = 0.0008$.

The total intensity for light with a more general spectral distribution $S(\lambda)$, such as that shown by the heavy broken line in Fig. 4.4(a), corresponds to the area under the broken line. The X, Y, and Z tristimulus values for this $S(\lambda)$ are obtained by the areas under the products of $S(\lambda)$ and the three matching functions $\bar{x}(\lambda), \bar{y}(\lambda)$, and $\bar{z}(\lambda)$. These products are shown as the red, green, and blue regions in Fig. 4.4(b). The X, Y, and Z tristimulus values that correspond to these shaded areas (i.e. the integrals) under the curves are {0.0065, 0.0087, 0.0069}.

Although the X, Y, Z values do give a complete representation of the color, for many purposes, color scientists have found it more convenient to divide the values of X, Y, Z by the intensity and then display colors using only two, $\{u, v\}$, out of a set of three, $\{u, v, w\}$, chromaticity coordinates. They are defined by dividing X, Y, Z by the intensity given by the sum $X + Y + Z$, as shown in Eq. 4.3. The colors displayed in this way are shown on the two-dimensional *horseshoe map* in Fig. 4.5. Note that since they are calculated by dividing by $X + Y + Z$, their sum $u + v + w = 1$, and only the two $\{u, v\}$ are necessary to specify the color. This horseshoe-shaped area,

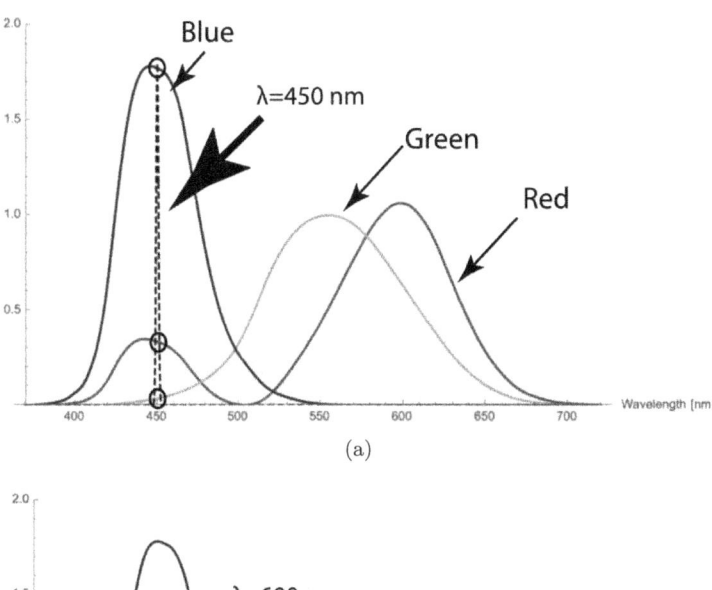

Fig. 4.3. Illustration of how the color coordinates for $\lambda = 450$ and 600 nm are obtained from the CIE color matching functions.

which is known as the *gamut* of color vision, contains all of the colors that the human eye can see:[2]

$$u = X/(X + Y + Z), \quad v = Y/(X + Y + Z), \quad w = Z/(X + Y + Z).$$
$$(4.3)$$

---

[2]Note that the colors in Fig. 4.5 are only symbolic since the printed page cannot display the true values.

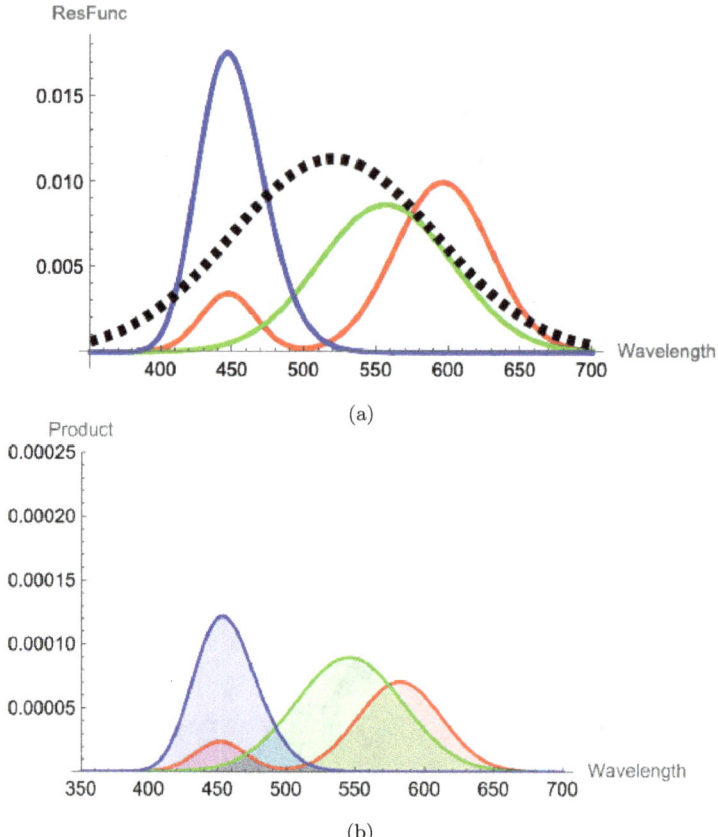

Fig. 4.4. (a) The red, green, and blue $\bar{x}(\lambda), \bar{y}(\lambda)$, and $\bar{z}(\lambda)$ matching functions shown along with one typical light signal that is shown by the heavy broken line. (b) The three curves that show the overlap between the light signal and the matching functions. The areas under these three curves correspond to the XYZ tristimulus values.

The numbers on the outside of the curved upper border indicate all the colors that are produced with *single wavelengths* of light. All the colors in the interior of the horseshoe, as well as those on the straight line at the bottom, can only be formed by some mixture of other colors.

The $\{u, v\}$ chromaticity values for light of wavelength 450 nm can be shown from the above X, Y, and Z to be $\{u, v\} = \{0.16, 0.02\}$ and for 600 nm to be {0.63, 0.37}. These are displayed as black circles on the border of the horseshoe. The chromaticity coordinates for $S(\lambda)$ displayed in Fig. 4.4 are obtained by dividing the tristimulus values $X, Y, Z = (0.0065, 0.0087, 0.006)$ by the sum $X + Y + Z = 0.0212$. The results are $\{u, v\} = \{0.31, 0.41\}$ along with $w = 1 - u - v = 0.28$. This point is shown as the black star in Fig. 4.5.

The small black hexagon at $\{u, v\} = \{0.33, 0.33\}$ corresponds to the color white that nominally occurs with $X = Y = Z$. These values for white correspond to the overlap between the CIE color

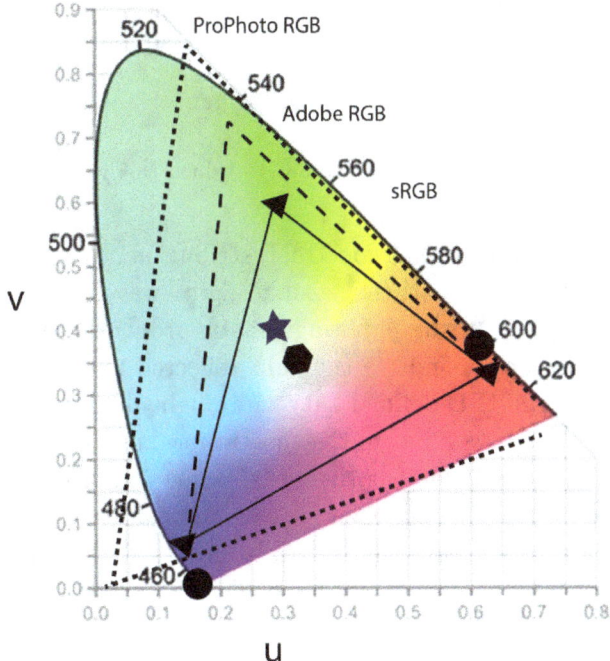

Fig. 4.5. CIE chromaticity diagram: The points *corresponding* to $\lambda = 450$ and 600 nm are marked by the black dots on the border. The white point, as explained in the text, is shown by the hexagon. The small solid black triangles indicate the primaries ($\lambda = 465, 555,$ and 610 nm) that define the vertices of what is known as the s*RGB* color space, also to be explained. The larger triangle with these vertices displays the s*RGB* color space. The other larger triangles (Adobe *RGB*, ProPhotoRGB) display bigger *RGB* color spaces, which are explained in Section 4.4. The black star indicates $\{u, v\}$ for the light spectra $S(\lambda)$, drawn as the heavy dashed line in Fig. 4.4.

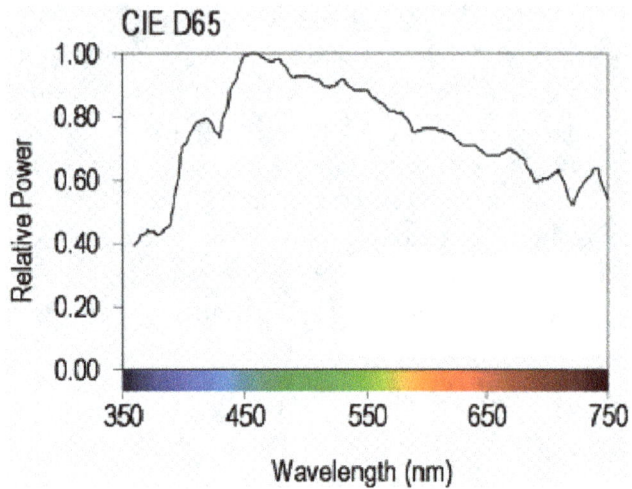

Fig. 4.6. Spectrum $S(\lambda)$ of the CIE-defined D65 white light.

matching function and a flat spectral distribution $S(\lambda)$ that contains equal amounts of all of the visible light wavelengths. In this diagram, it happens to be indistinguishable from $\{u,\ v\} = \{0.3128,\ 0.3290\}$, which corresponds to the light reflected from a whiteboard illuminated by the CIE-defined D65 white light illuminant shown in Fig. 4.6. This $S(\lambda)$ is similar to the spectra for daylight that is shown in Fig. 4.7. Although they both fall off somewhat for wavelengths shorter than about 450 nm, their relative intensities are comparable for all of the visible wavelengths. As a practical matter, both the fluorescent and incandescent spectra will also appear white to most eyes. As discussed further in Section 4.3, all of these spectra would appear white to most observers even though they do not strictly satisfy $X = Y = Z$.

4.2 Quantitative Color Display

In actuality, virtually all color displays are created from a superposition of three primary colors. In a manner that is similar to the way the CIE color space can be defined in terms of the three tristimulus values $X,\ Y,\ Z$, these primaries define what are referred

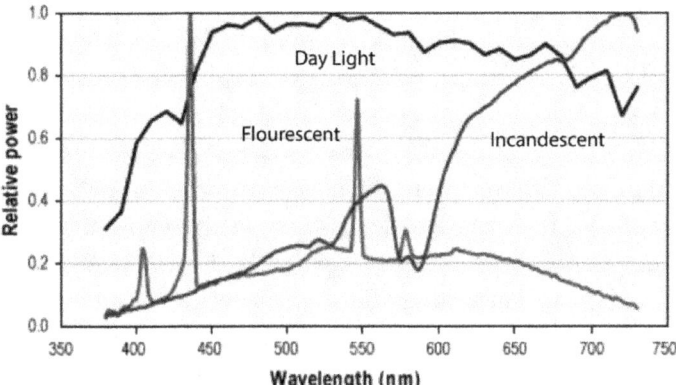

Fig. 4.7. Examples of spectral power distribution $S(\lambda)$ for daylight, fluorescent light, and incandescent light. Note that compared to the daylight $S(\lambda)$, the incandescent spectra are richer in the red, and the fluorescent contains spikes at two or three wavelengths that are characteristic of the gas in the fluorescent tube.

to as *RGB color spaces*. The small solid black triangles in Fig. 4.5, corresponding to 465, 555, and 610 nm, indicate the chromaticity values of the primaries for the s*RGB* color space. This s*RGB* color space is displayed as a triangle with these vertices. This is the color space that is employed in nearly all liquid crystal displays (LCDs). The area inside the triangle contains the chromaticity values for all of the colors that can be produced by linear combinations of these primaries. The colors outside the s*RGB* triangle can only be approximated using a process known as *rendering intent*.[3]

For display purposes, the intensities of the primaries are typically specified by 8-bit binary numbers varying from 0 to $255 = (2^8 - 1)$. The values of 255 produce the maximum intensity for the display primaries. This corresponds to $255 \times 255 \times 255 = 16,581,375$ colors. In view of the fact that the bit depth of the RAW data is often larger

---

[3]One type of rendering intent referred to as *perceptual* simply shrinks all the color values to fall inside the s*RGB* triangle. Another intent known as *relative colorimetric* just moves the color values to the nearest point on the perimeter of the s*RGB* triangle.

than 8 bits, the raw data must be scaled down by either the camera or computer processor.

4.3 Human Color Vision

The principal difference between the discussion in the previous section and the way we see color is that our perception of color from any small region in an image varies with the colors of neighboring regions. This very surprising fact was dramatically demonstrated in an article in *Scientific American* by E. H. Land.[4] The essence of the demonstration makes use of two identical arrays of color patches and two sets of three illuminating lights with three different wavelengths. For one array, the intensities of three illuminating wavelengths are chosen, and as expected, a white patch appears white and a green patch looks green. The intensities of the light reflected from this white patch were recorded. For the second array, the illuminating intensities are adjusted so that the light reflected from the green patch is identical to the intensities of the light reflected from the white patch in the first array. If the perceived color were solely determined by the wavelengths of the reflected light, the green patch would have appeared white; however, the surprise is that the colors of both arrays appear identical. The white and green patches look the same on both arrays, despite the differences in the reflected spectra. This effect, in which colors are perceived on the basis of neighboring colors rather than the wavelengths of the illuminating light, is known as *color constancy*, which was introduced near the close of Section 1.3 of Chapter 1.

The *Munker* illusion, as displayed in Fig. 4.8, is a demonstration of the opposite form in which two images appear to be different even though both the light illuminating them and the reflected light have the same spectral distributions. The gray shades in column (a) appear darker than those in (b), even though they have identical chromaticity and intensities. This effect, which arises from the same

---

[4]Land E. H. *Retinex Theory of Color-Vision*. Scientific American, 1977; 237(6):108.

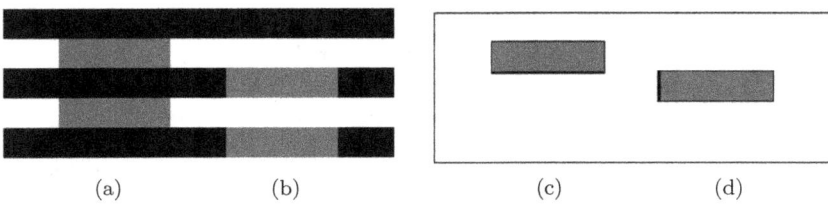

Fig. 4.8. Illustration of the *Munker* illusion: Although they appear different, all three gray bars in (a) and (b) have identical chromaticity and intensities. When the black bars are removed, one can see that the gray regions in (c) and (d) are identical.

perceptual properties as color constancy, occurs because what we perceive is based on some sort of average over the light in neighboring regions rather than from a single point. This is true so long as the illuminate covers a reasonably wide range of wavelengths. Reiterating the above, it turns out that our visual system perceives colors through a process that interprets what is being seen by comparing adjacent colors. For the effect in Fig. 4.8, our vision compares the gray shade in each column to the adjacent black or white bars. One can convince oneself that the gray shaded regions are identical by comparing the gray bands in (c) and (d), for which the adjacent black regions in (a) and (b) have been removed. The gray shades in all four columns are identical.[5]

The problem for photography is that digital cameras record the intensities of an image differently from the way we perceive them. A digital camera records the colors at a single point without regard to the neighboring colors. Thus, if a picture is taken in bright sunlight at midday, the recorded colors would be different from the same picture taken in the late afternoon, when the illuminating colors are redder since the sun is near to setting. In contrast, our eyes don't really perceive a difference in the scene. If one wants the photographs taken under different conditions to appear the same as the way the scene is viewed by the eye, the cameras or computers need to be

---

[5]One can also convince oneself of this by making a mask by cutting holes in a piece of paper and masking the regions surrounding the gray bars.

given specific instructions to correct for this effect. The way this is done, which is called *white balance*, is discussed in Section 4.8.

To summarize the message from this section:

Color constancy: Reflected images can appear identical even though the illuminating wavelengths are different.

Even with the same illuminating wavelengths, different spots on an image can appear different if the neighboring colors are different.

Metamerism: The same colors can be produced by different wavelengths.

4.4 Color Spaces

Before moving on, we want to return to the CIE chromaticity diagram in Fig. 4.5. To reiterate what was said above, various combinations of the three s*RGB* primaries marked by the vertices of the s*RGB* triangle in Fig. 4.5 can be combined to produce any of the colors within the triangle. This is standard for most computer monitors, printers, and web applications. There are other *RGB* color spaces, such as those displayed in Fig. 4.5, that are larger than s*RGB*. These are typically used in various editing applications to bring out features in the image that would otherwise be obscured by the constraints of s*RGB*. On the other hand, these editing processes must eventually map the edited parts of the images to the smaller s*RGB* format to be viewed by conventional monitors or printers.

The point to bear in mind is that, regardless of the area of these different *RGB* color spaces, most of them are 8 bit. That is, each of the three colors can only have any of the $(0, 1, 2, 3, \ldots, 255)$, or $2^8 - 1$, levels of intensity. To repeat the point made in Section 4.2, when these colors are combined, the *RGB* spaces can display $(2^8 - 1) \times (2^8 - 1) \times (2^8 - 1) \sim 16.6$ million colors. More will be said about the differences between different file types in Chapter 5; however, for now, one should be aware that the RAW-type image files in different cameras can record anywhere from 12 to 16 bits of the number of shades of colors. Thus, RAW files can contain considerably more colors than can be displayed on conventional monitors or printers that rely on an 8-bit s*RGB* color space. Nevertheless, most professionals and advanced amateurs often prefer to edit their images in file formats that have larger bit depths, such as TIFF. The reason for this is that it makes it possible to enhance or suppress different parts of the image. More will be said about the advantages and disadvantages of TIFF versus JPEG in Chapter 5.

For completeness, it is worth mentioning that a second color model that is used in the JPEG conversion is the *YCrCb* color model. In this model, the value of the *Y* coordinate specifies the brightness of the pixel, while the values of *Cr* and *Cb* specify the relative values of red to green and blue to green, respectively. This model more easily corresponds to the way colors are viewed by our eyes.[6] A few of the most commonly used color spaces are listed in Table 4.1. Each of these provides a specific organization of colors that are employed in different devices. They will not be discussed further; however, the interested reader can find more on Wikipedia.

Table 4.1. List of some of the color spaces in common usage.

Additive Color Spaces	
CIE XYZ	Color space based on measurements of human color perception
RGB	Common color spaces that are used for creation and editing of computer and print images
YCbCr	Additive color space used in color image pipeline for JPEG compression
Subtractive Color Space	
CMYK	Subtractive color space used in printing

---

[6]The colors displayed using additive color spaces, such as RGB, are produced by the superposition of light from red, green, and blue primaries. Thus, the color yellow is the result of adding red and green lights. Printers, on the other hand, more commonly use a CMYK color model that describes the way colors are produced using a subtraction process. In the subtraction process, the ink for a yellow image, for example, absorbs (or subtracts) blue light such that when illuminated with white light, only red and green are reflected.

Finally, we point out one possible artifact that can occur if the additional bit depth of the RAW data is used to excessively enhance the contrast in an image beyond the 8-bit capacity of sRGB. The artifact known as *banding* occurs if the gradual contrast available with the larger bit space and cannot be reproduced by the smaller 8-bit display. In this case, the gradual color gradations of the larger bit space are replaced by *steps* in color shades. Interested readers can view examples of banding effects on Wikipedia.

4.5 Camera Bayer to Computer RGB

As was mentioned above, digital cameras record the measured color intensity for each point in the image as it is projected onto the Bayer array *without any processing.* The issue that needs to be described is the details of how the camera determines the X, Y, and Z tristimulus values for each point in the image and how these are translated into the RGB color data that the computer knows how to display.

As might be implied from above the tristimulus X, Y, and Z values in the camera are obtained from the overlap of the spectral distribution of the light incident with the spectral response distributions of the three color Bayer filters, as shown in Fig. 4.9. This is basically the same way the X, Y, Z values were defined in the discussion in Section 4.1.[7] The X, Y, and Z values obtained from the response functions in Fig. 4.9 for the different pixels in the Bayer array make up the basic RAW image to be transmitted to a processor in a computer.

As was already mentioned, since the RGB color spaces are the ones used for most computer processing, the X, Y, Z color values stored as RAW need to be converted to the 8-bit RGB color space by which color is produced for computer displays. The complication of this is that since each of the Bayer pixels has only one color filter, i.e. only one of the three response functions in Fig. 4.9, the different tristimulus values from the different pixels, which arise from

---

[7]The distributions vary with the camera manufacturer.

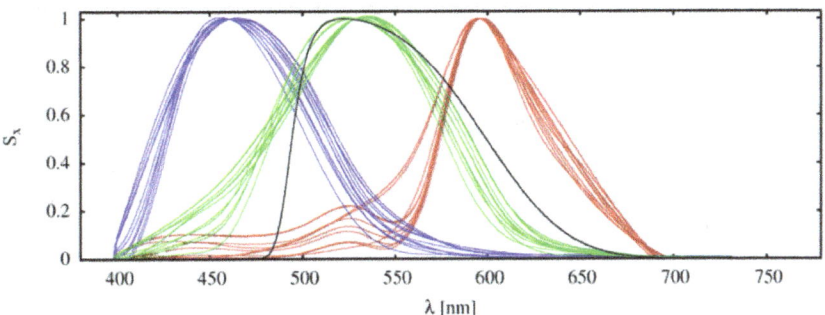

Fig. 4.9. Typical spectral response functions of the three color filters for cameras with *RGB* bands. The black solid line shows a response band that is used in astronomical devices.

slightly different points in the image, must somehow be combined. The *demosaicing* process for doing this is the subject of the following section.

4.6 Demosaicing

There are two things that need to be considered before the RAW color data recorded in the Bayer array are translated into a useful image. The first is that the Bayer array contains twice as many sensors for green as for red and blue. The reason for this is that the intensity recorded by the green sensors is a better measure of the image brightness than that recorded by the red and blue ones. It turns out that our eyes are more sensitive to small changes in brightness than to small changes in color, and half as many red and blue records are perfectly adequate for good color interpretation. The consequence of this is that if the image of the unprocessed image was viewed directly, it would be too green. The second thing that needs to be dealt with is that the directly viewed image would have color artifacts because the red, green, and blue images are physically separate pixels. This must be contrasted with the display, computer, or print, for which each pixel or image point must have the information for all three colors. The translation from the camera to display colors is known as *demosaicing*.

Since response curves, such as those in Fig. 4.9, vary with camera manufacturers, the algorithms for converting the Bayer records to a computer-useable color space are also different for different cameras. Nevertheless, they all have methods by which the colors on neighboring pixels are averaged in order to assign to each computer pixel three binary numbers, R, G, and B, for the designated RGB color space (or color profile). A schematic illustration of a simplified version of the demosaicing process is illustrated in Fig. 4.10.

The LCD diagram on the right shows a 3×3 section of display pixels, showing the three light-emitting color diodes that make up the illumination from each pixel on a computer display. The RGB values for the intensity of each display pixel are assigned three numbers that are suitable averages of the recorded intensities in the corresponding neighboring Bayer pixels. In this case, which is an oversimplification of the real process, the color values of red and blue that are assigned to the central display pixel are the average of the values in the neighboring red and blue Bayer pixels that are outlined with heavy broken lines. As was explained in Section 3.7 of Chapter 3, digital cameras often give users the option of saving images as either an

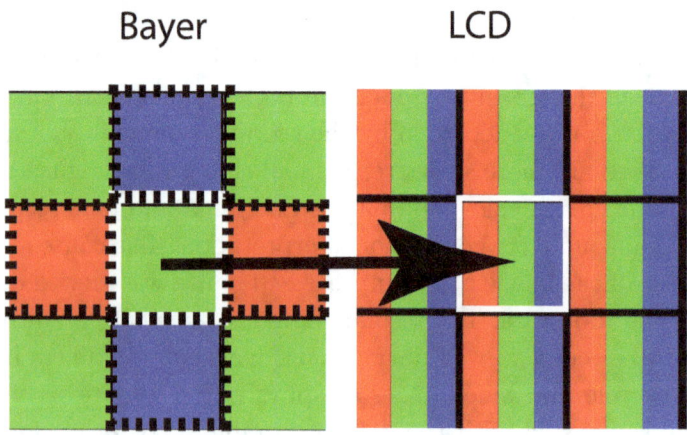

Fig. 4.10. Schematic illustration of the Bayer to liquid crystal pixel transformation.

unprocessed RAW or a demosaiced TIFF file[8] that contains all of the same information as the RAW file but is at least three times larger since each image pixel has three times more data. Alternatively, the data can be saved in a significantly smaller JPEG file. Compressed JPEG files of varying qualities can be significantly smaller; however, they have the advantage that they can both be immediately viewed on the camera or elsewhere with no further processing and/or sent by most email programs.

4.7 The Display Histograms

As should be clear from the previous sections, color instructions for the RGB color spaces employed by computer monitors consist of a triplet of numbers that specify the intensity of the R, G, and B primaries that are needed for each pixel. As was said above, for the most commonly used 8-bit displays, these number run from 0 to $255 \, (2^8 - 1)$.[9] White and all shades of gray are nominally obtained by values of $R = G = B$. The color content of any RGB image is conveniently summarized by what is known as a *histogram*. The picture on the left in Fig. 4.11 displays an underexposed image along with four histograms of the color distributions in this image. In each histogram, the horizontal axes represent the R, G, or B values of the image pixels. The vertical axes represent the number of pixels with each value of R, G, or B. As one might anticipate, there are virtually no pixels for the larger values of R, G, and B for the underexposed image. The vertical bars reflect the fact that the only pixels that contain non-zero values are those at the lower end of the RGB scale. In contrast, for the brighter version to the right, the number of pixels that have values for the higher number of R, G, and B pixels in the histograms in Fig. 4.11 is significantly greater. The goal of spreading out the histogram is one of the simplest objectives of image editing.

---

[8]TIFF files can also be compressed using a lossless algorithm that produces a somewhat smaller file.

[9]In view of the fact that the values for an 8-bit number start at 0, the largest value is $2^8 - 1 = 255$.

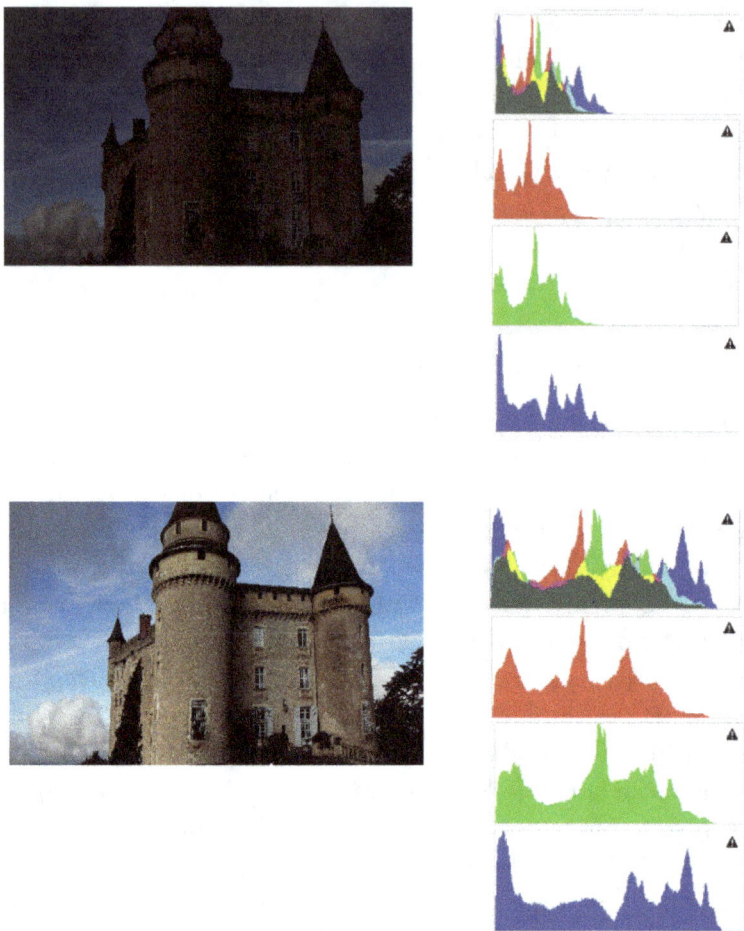

Fig. 4.11. Examples of an underexposed image (upper) and a correctly exposed image (lower) along with the color, red, green, and blue histograms for the two images.

4.8 White Balance

One issue that needs to be understood in color photography is how to deal with the *color constancy* effect that was demonstrated by Land and discussed in Section 4.3.[10] The point made there was that the

---

[10]Land E. H. *Retinex Theory of Color-Vision. Scientific American*, 1977; 237(6):108.

way color is perceived by the human visual system is different from the way colors are recorded by a camera. For example, the wavelength spectra $S(\lambda)_{\text{ref}}$ reflected from any object being photographed are the product of the spectra of the incident light $S(\lambda)_{\text{incid}}$ and the reflectance $\chi(\lambda)$ of the reflecting material:

$$S(\lambda)_{\text{ref}} = \chi(\lambda)S(\lambda)_{\text{incid}}. \tag{4.4}$$

For example, comparing the shapes of the incandescent and daylight spectral power densities $S(\lambda)_{\text{incid}}$ displayed in Fig. 4.7, one can see that the relative intensity of red wavelengths ($\lambda > 600\,\text{nm}$) for incandescent light is considerably larger than for the shorter wavelengths. This is not true for daylight.

The effect of this is that unless corrections are made, the histogram of the recorded colors of a photograph taken under incandescent light would have larger values in the red than one photographed in daylight. The effect of this is that computer-processed images taken with incandescent light would be redder than the equivalent image taken in sunlight. An example of this can be seen by comparing the two images in the upper portion of Fig. 4.12. The image on the upper left was exposed with a neutral $S(\lambda)_{\text{incid}}$ that has roughly equal intensities for all visible wavelengths. The image on the upper right was exposed with a *warmer* $S(\lambda)_{\text{incid}}$ whose intensities are skewed to be richer in red than the shorter wavelengths. The point that Land made and discussed in Section 4.3 is that although these two processed images are different, the colors of the original scenes as perceived by human vision would not have been different. This is the effect known as *color constancy*.

The two histograms in the lower portion of Fig. 4.12 display the histograms that illustrate the spectral distributions $S(\lambda)_{\text{ref}}$ of two images that were exposed to different light sources. Although the difference in the histograms is slight, it is clear that the one for the *warmer* image has slightly more intensity in the red than the one illuminated with a neutral $S(\lambda)_{\text{incid}}$. The challenge for photography is to apply corrections to the photographic processes such that pictures are the same as the original scene, regardless of $S(\lambda)_{\text{incid}}$. The steps by which the colors of photographic images are adjusted

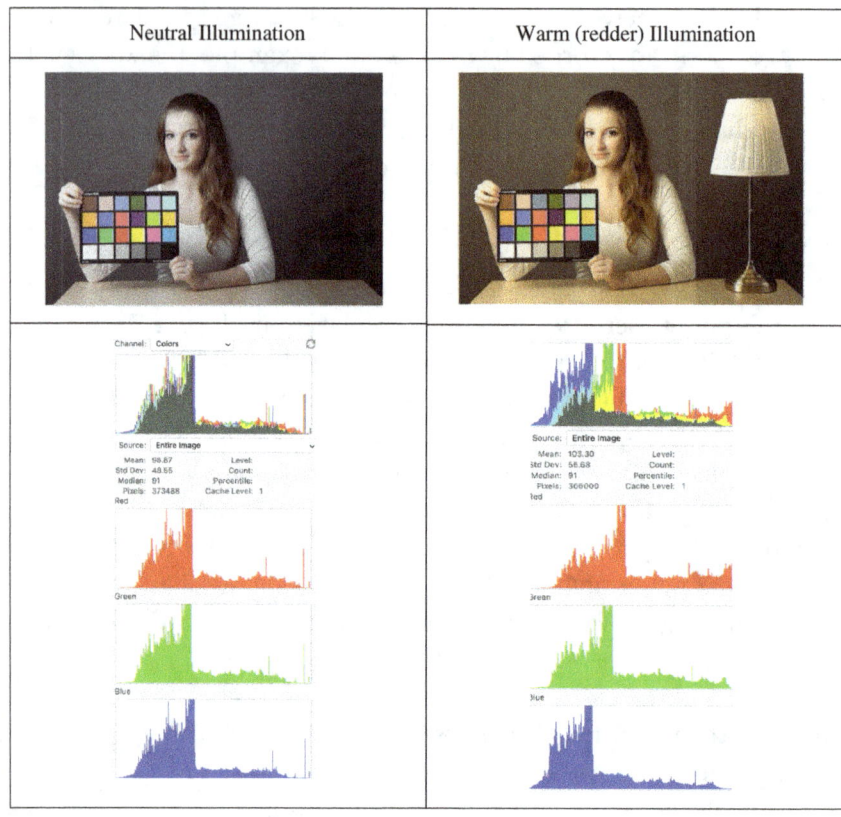

Fig. 4.12. Images showing the differences between photographs exposed to white light and a warmer, i.e. redder, light source. The histograms in the lower portion are only very slightly different, but one can see that the one on the right side has slightly more intensity in the red.

in response to variations in the spectral power distributions of the illuminating light are known as *white balancing*. As was mentioned when discussing image *pipelines* (Section 3.1 of Chapter 3), this can be done in the camera during exposure or during computer processing of RAW images, as explained in the following chapter.

Chapter 5

RAW, TIFF, and JPEG File Types

5.1 RAW

As already mentioned, images saved in the RAW format preserve all the information in the original image. This leaves the user with the maximum flexibility for subsequent processing. Perhaps the most important freedom is the white-balancing option that was just referred to. Although most cameras give the user the option to either manually select the illuminant for the exposure (i.e. daylight, cloudy, fluorescent, etc.) or have the camera do it automatically, one of the most important advantages of RAW is that it provides the user with the ability to easily select a white-balance choice on the computer that is different from the one made in the camera at the time of taking the photograph. For example, Fig. 5.1 illustrates the white-balance choices that are available when opening a RAW file using Adobe Photoshop. With Photoshop, this must be done during the opening process since once converted to either JPEG or TIFF, the white balance can only be corrected by a manual operation, which makes it rather difficult to select color choices that achieve accurate reproduction of subtleties in image colors.

These computer color adjustments for white-balance options, such as daylight to incandescent, involve straightforward scaling of the recorded red, green, and blue intensities according to the known differences in the illuminants. On the other hand, it is also possible to allow the software on the computer to make the adjustment automatically. There are two common ways in which the *automatic* adjustment is done. The first method assumes that the average of

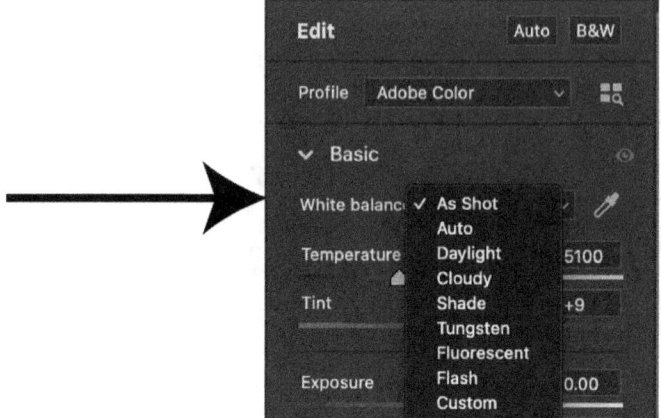

Fig. 5.1. Screenshot of the *white balance* menu options that are available when opening a RAW document in Adobe Photoshop.

all of the colors in a given image are achromatic (i.e. the average color is gray). The second method assumes that the brightest area in the image is white. To implement the first method, the computer or camera calculates the numerical average values $\langle R \rangle$, $\langle G \rangle$, and $\langle B \rangle$ of the R_{sensor}, G_{sensor}, and B_{sensor} numbers of all the pixels in the image and scales the corresponding values in each pixel such that the average values for the final image are equal. This is done by setting the image values for the red, green, and blue pixels to be $R_{\text{image}} = K(R_{\text{sensor}}/\langle R_{\text{sensor}} \rangle), G_{\text{image}} = K(G_{\text{sensor}}/\langle G_{\text{sensor}} \rangle)$, and $B_{\text{image}} = K(B_{\text{sensor}}/\langle B_{\text{sensor}} \rangle)$, with $K = \langle G_{\text{image}} \rangle$. With this scaling, the average image values $\langle R_{\text{image}} \rangle = \langle G_{\text{image}} \rangle = \langle B_{\text{image}} \rangle$ are all equal to K.

The implementation in the second method is done by a similar scaling in which $\langle R_{\text{sensor}} \rangle$, $\langle G_{\text{sensor}} \rangle$, and $\langle B_{\text{sensor}} \rangle$ are replaced by R_{max}, G_{max}, and B_{max}, with $K = G_{\text{max}}$.

Although most users are quite happy with the white-balance choices built into either the camera or the RAW software options, such as those shown in Fig. 5.1, one should be aware of products such as *colorchecker/PASSPORT PHOTO* that allow the user to produce a color profile for the camera that is specific to the illuminating conditions at the time of taking the photograph.

5.2 TIFF

The process that converts from RAW to TIFF preserves all of the information in the original image; however, by virtue of demosaicing, in which each display pixel has data for each of the three colors, the TIFF files are of the order of three times larger than the original RAW. There is no question that many people feel that the price paid for these large files is justified by the more flexible editing possibilities; however, others argue that the differences between the TIFF and the much smaller JPEG, which is discussed in the following section, do not warrant the larger files. Eventually, each user will have to decide for themselves whether the size differences is important.

One example of the difference between editing in TIFF and JPEG is illustrated in Fig. 5.2. The images in (a) are TIFF (left) and JPEG (right) severely underexposed images of a house. The image in (b) is the same image after the TIFF file has been edited to enhance the brightness. In fact, it would be hard to see the subtle differences between either the edited TIFF or JPEG image (not shown) at the displayed magnification. On the other hand, (c) illustrates that there are significant visible differences at high magnification between the TIFF (left) and JPEG (right) images. The differences in the pixel distributions in the histograms (d) and (e) for these two images are apparent. The intensity distribution of the JPEG histogram (e) has a *"spikey"* character that is not present in the TIFF histogram (d).

One advantage of editing in the TIFF format, which is also true of JPEG, is that, in contrast to RAW files, TIFF and JPEG are both common graphic image formats that can be read on almost any computer platform. Finally, once the editing of a TIFF file is complete, it is customary to export the images to the smaller JPEG format for sharing via email or other methods. On the other hand, others simply have the camera save images as JPEG, bypassing the RAW/TIFF steps.

One additional advantage of editing in TIFF rather than in JPEG is that it is a *lossless* process which preserves all the information in the original image. In contrast, the editing and saving that are done on JPEG files discards information in what is basically a lossy process. As was already mentioned, the differences between JPEG

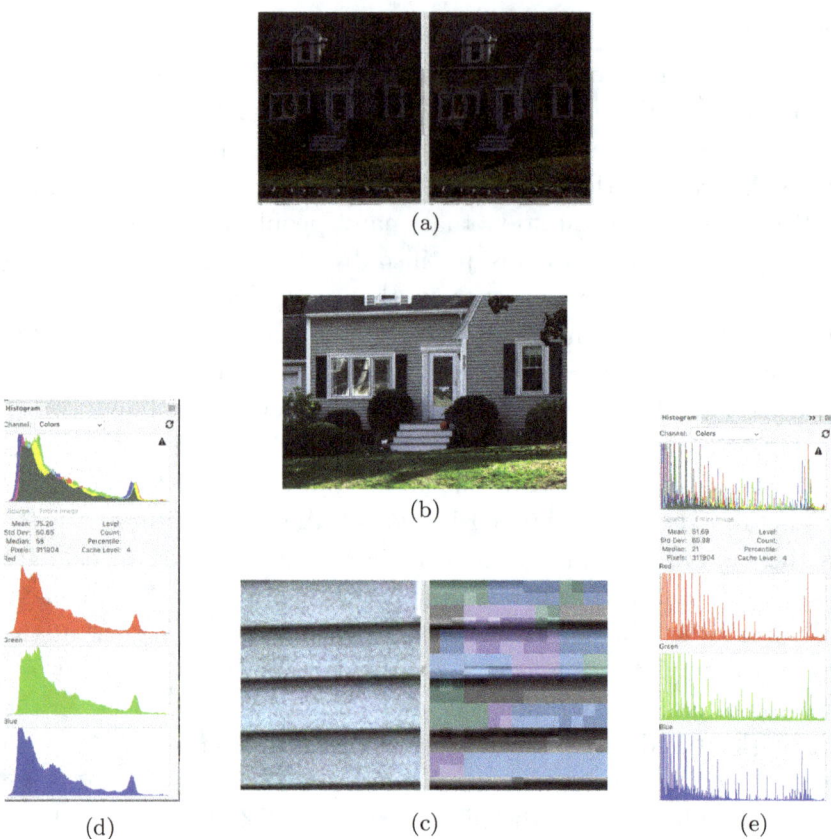

Fig. 5.2. Illustration comparing TIFF and JPEG files: (a) Underexposed TIFF and low-quality JPEG. (b) Either image edited to increase exposure. The difference between TIFF and JPEG would not be observable at this magnification. (c) Visible differences between magnified versions of the edited versions of TIFF and JPEG. (d and e) Histograms of the edited versions of TIFF and JPEG.

and TIFF may not be obvious to many users, but they are there if needed. Finally, if size is an issue, it is worth noting that TIFF files can be copied to a smaller compressed TIFF form that uses a lossless algorithm but preserves all of the information of the original RAW/TIFF files. Nevertheless, the smaller files produced by the lossless TIFF reduction are still considerably larger than even the highest-quality JPEG files.

5.3 JPEG

Whether the JPEG compression is done in the camera or as an output choice following editing of a TIFF file, the compression process is basically identical.[1] The JPEG compression process relies on the fact that our visual perception is much more sensitive to variations in the intensity of an image than to variations in the color information. In order to take advantage of this feature, color scientists developed the $YCbCr$ color space mentioned in Section 4.4 of Chapter 4, in which the Y component contains the intensity information while the Cb and Cr contain the chrominance (i.e. the color) information. Although the coordinates of the RGB color space contain the same color information as the $YCbCr$ coordinates, the latter turn out to be better suited for the data compression that removes information not needed for visual color perception. The mathematical transformation by which the triplet of RGB numbers is mapped onto the $YCbCr$ triplet is beyond the scope of what we want to discuss here.

JPEG compression takes place in three steps. The first that we just mentioned is the conversion of the combination of intensity and $\{u, v\}$ coordinates of the RGB color space into the coordinates for the $YCbCr$ color space. The second step is to reduce the amount of the stored $CbCr$ data in a way that preserves the visual image without loss of image quality. As was mentioned above, since our visual system is less sensitive to color variations than to intensity variations, the image quality is not compromised by reducing the number of pixels needed to record the $CbCr$ data by a factor of 4 (i.e. $1/4 = (1/2) \times (1/2)$. Thus, if the size of the original image had $N = N_{Cb}N_{Cr}$ pixels in all three of the $YCbCr$ channels, this step reduces the size of the Cb and Cr channels to $N_R = (N_{Cb}/2)(N_{Cr}/2)$ channels. The third step is to further reduce the amount of stored data in a way that minimizes redundant information. For example, the amount of data that is needed to record the gradual change from, say, dark to light blue depends on both the amplitude of the change and the number of pixels over which the change occurs. The way

---

[1]The quality of JPEG conversion can vary between low and high quality. The choice of quality determines the size of the JPEG file. See Table 3.4.

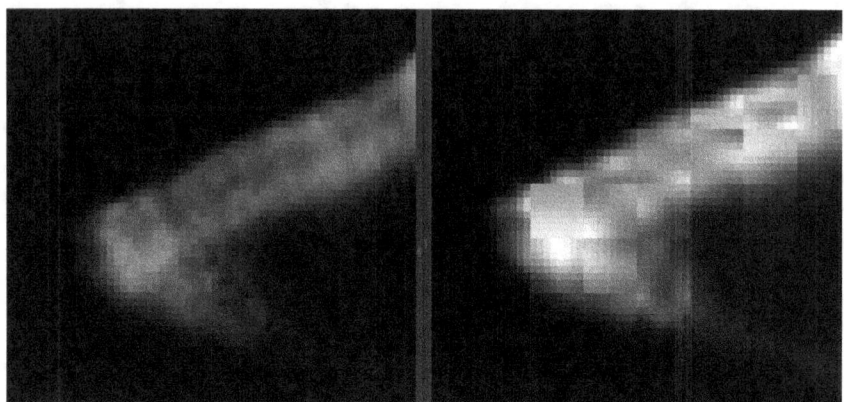

Fig. 5.3. Comparison between small sections of high- and low-quality JPEG compressions that have been enlarged by a factor of 3200% in order to visualize the display pixels. The image on the right shows the 8 × 8 blocks that are used for JPEG compression but which can't be seen in the high-quality compression.

that this works is that the JPEG compression breaks the image into sections of 8 × 8 pixels. Within each of these blocks, the algorithm smooths out the data in adjacent pixels such that differences in the color of adjacent pixels that are too small to be perceived by our eyes are removed. Aside from the size difference shown in Table 3.4, the quality differences between high- and low-quality compressed JPEG files is illustrated in Fig. 5.3 by a highly magnified section of a black-and-white image. First, note that in the low-quality JPEG on the right, the 8 × 8 sections mentioned above are visible. Second, note that within each of the 8 × 8 sections in the low-quality JPEG image, the relatively small texture variations in the high-quality JPEG are washed out. Although we don't show it here, the point, as implied earlier, is that it would be very hard to display on the printed page any difference between the highest-quality JPEG files and the TIFF files. The user will have to decide for themselves about the differences between the higher- and lower-quality versions of their images. The important point is that the smaller size of JPEG is advantageous for a number of reasons, including the sending of images electronically or posting on the internet.

Chapter 6

The Viewfinder

Virtually every digital camera has an LCD on its rear for viewing and framing the scene to be shot. While these are convenient, they have two disadvantages that are overcome by eye-level viewers, which are described in the following. Their principal disadvantage is that it is difficult to see the display in the presence of very bright ambient light. The second disadvantage has to do with the effect of camera shake, which is explained at the close of Section 7.1.2 of Chapter 7.

The three most common types of eye-level viewers are schematically illustrated in Fig. 6.1. The optical viewfinder labeled (a) was typically built into low-end point-and-shoot film cameras and is still available in compact *rangefinder* cameras, as well as a secondary viewer in cameras that have the type (b) viewfinder. The viewfinder type (a) has an optical path that is completely separate from the main image forming optics. The arrow illustrates the direct light path to the *optical viewer*. Its three advantages are as follows: (i) It can be viewed in bright ambient light; (2) it does not require battery power and can be used when the camera is not activated; and (3) the camera shake effects mentioned at the end of Section 7.1.2 of Chapter 7 can be reduced by holding the camera against the face while exposing.

The viewfinder type (b) was typical of virtually all film single-lens reflex (SLR) cameras. They are still common on many *digital single-lens reflex* (DSLR) cameras. For viewing, the mirror in front of the sensor deflects the light from the scene to the *pentaprism* above. The reason for the prism is that, as shown in Fig. 2.2, the image from the main lens is *upside down*. The pentaprism flips the

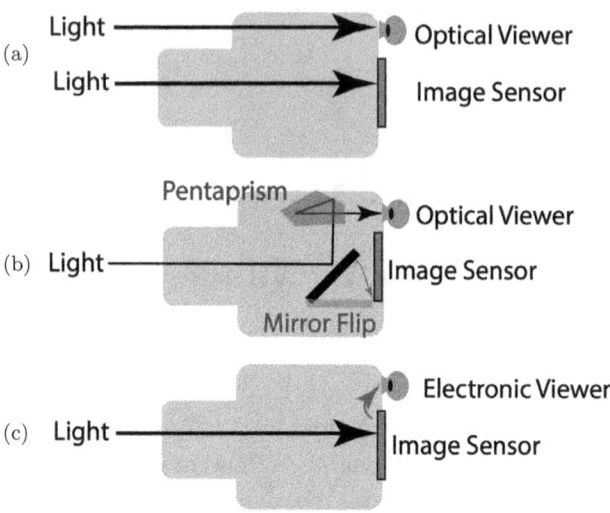

Fig. 6.1. Schematic illustration of the primary optics of the three most common eye-level viewers in digital cameras that are discussed in the text.

image so that the image in the optical viewer is right side up. When the shutter is activated, the mirror flips out of the way to allow the light to reach the sensor. Viewer (b) shares two of the advantages of (a) in that it can be employed without drawing battery power and used in bright ambience. Although the shake effects of cameras with (b) can be minimized by holding them against the face, this advantage is compromised by vibrations that can be induced by the motion of flipping the mirror. The time to displace the mirror also slightly delays the time of the exposure. Furthermore, similar to the disadvantages that are discussed for mechanical shutters in Section 7.1.2 of Chapter 7, all devices involving mechanical motions are susceptible to noise, wear, and breakage.

The viewer of type (c) has become increasingly common in what are generally referred to as *mirrorless* cameras. In general, they are more compact and weigh less than the comparable DSLRs with type (b) viewfinders. With fewer moving parts, mirrorless cameras are quieter and less susceptible to shaking, wear, and breakage. A secondary advantage is that mirrorless cameras can usually have faster shutter speeds than comparable DSLRs. In addition, the electronic viewer provides the same true live view, although smaller, as the image on the larger LCD. This allows the operator to adjust the exposure settings before snapping the picture. The main downside of the mirrorless camera is that the result of the electrical current drawn by the electronic viewer is responsible for shorter battery life.

Chapter 7

Effects of Shooting Settings

The first of the two principal objectives of this section is to describe the controls that photographers have at their disposal for managing the exposure, or brightness, of an image. In the predigital era, it was possible to select films of varying sensitivity or *speed*. Once the film *speed* was selected, the only two choices available for varying the image brightness were the aperture size, i.e. $f/\#$ (Section 7.1.1), and shutter speed, Δt (Section 7.1.2). With digital cameras, users have a third available option of adjusting the ISO setting in order to vary the camera *sensitivity* (Section 7.1.3).[1] Once the ISO setting is set, either manually or automatically, virtually all cameras give users the option of exposing the image in one of the *shooting modes* described in Table 7.1.

A second objective in this section is to explain the secondary effects that accompany the camera settings. In addition to the brightness adjustments, digital cameras have the possibility of electronically magnifying, or *zooming*, an image. The pros and cons of digital versus optical zoom are discussed in Section 7.2. Finally, we comment on how an effect known as *perspective*, which describes the spatial relationship between different objects in an image, is influenced by the object distance rather than the lens focal length.

---

[1]The ISO setting is another way to vary the system gain (SG), see Eq. (3.8) in Section 3.5 of Chapter 3.

Table 7.1. Typical choices that users have when shooting an image is to select the *shooting* or *exposure* mode. The camera sensitivity, or ISO, is set manually for each mode.

Exposure Modes		Shutter Speed (Δt)	Aperture ($f/\#$)	Properties
Mode P	Programmed Auto	Camera	Camera	Camera automatically adjusts exposure
Mode S	Shutter Priority	User	Camera	Camera adjusts $f/\#$ following user's choice of Δt
Mode A	Aperture Priority	Camera	User	Camera adjusts Δt following user's choice of $f/\#$
Mode M	Manual	User	User	User adjusts exposure

(Chooser (Camera or User) spans the Shutter Speed and Aperture columns.)

7.1 Brightness Controls

The standard process for optimizing image brightness is to try to choose the diameter of the lens aperture ($f/\#$) and the length of exposure time (Δt) such that the number of electrons stored in the brightest pixel in the image is approximately equal to the full well maximum of that pixel.[2] As was explained in Section 3.3 using Eq. (3.5) in Chapter 3, the amount of light passing through the lens is proportional to $(f/\#)^2$, which scales as the area of the lens. The exposure itself is therefore proportional to $(f/\#)^2\Delta t$, where Δt is the duration the shutter is open for exposure. If the exposure is sufficient to achieve the full well maximum number of stored electrons, the camera ADU (Section 3.5 of Chapter 3) will convert this amount of charge to a digital number that is well matched to the digital capacity of the camera computer. Fortunately, when there is not enough light to reach the full well maximum, digital cameras can

---

[2]This usually applies to the green pixels since they are a better measure of intensity than the red, green, or blue pixels. Remember, as was explained following Eq. (3.3), since the ratio of the lens diameter to f_{equiv} in cameras with smaller sensors is smaller than the lens diameter/f_{true}, the $f/\#$ must be defined as lens diameter/f_{true}.

make use of the ISO setting to enhance the conversion such that this same digital number can be achieved for a smaller number of stored electrons.[3] In this section, we explain how the image brightness can be maintained by selecting combinations of these three controls in order to achieve a satisfactory final image.

The trade-off in these three settings that produce the same brightness is conveniently described using the *exposure triangle*, which is illustrated in the upper portion of Fig. 7.1. Although it is somewhat confusing, this triangle is constructed using the three overlapping grids that are illustrated in the lower portion of Fig. 7.1. Three exposure examples are marked by the points A, B, and C. The grid on the lower left is designed to display the range of aperture, or $f/\#$, choices. The lengths of the broken lines from these points that run perpendicular to the grid, extending from the points to the triangle side marked *Aperture Base*, correspond to the $(f/\#)^2$ values of $f/4$ for point A and $f/8$ for points B and C. Note that the size of the aperture opening is proportional to $(f/\#)^2$ and the grid spacings correspond to factors of 2 in exposure. The grid displayed in the center of the lower part of the figure, making an angle of $60°$ to the aperture grid, is designed to display factors of 2 in shutter speed. The lines perpendicular to the side labeled *Shutter Speed Base* running from A, B, and C indicate shutter speeds of $1/125$ and $1/30$ of a second. The grid on the lower right is designed to display factors of 2 in ISO setting. The ISO settings for points A and B are the nominal values of 100, while the value for C is the enhanced sensitivity value of 400. The usefulness of these three grids derives from the fact that, for all three grids, the sum of the three perpendicular lengths from A, B, and C is equal. The effect of this, which will be proven in Section 8.3 of Chapter 8, is that the brightness BS of the exposure, given by Eq. (7.1), has the same value for every point in the exposure triangle:

$$\text{BS} \propto (f/\#)^2(\Delta t)(\text{ISO}). \tag{7.1}$$

This is demonstrated in Table 7.2 for the three points A, B, and C.

---

[3]As mentioned above, ISO adjustments are essentially the same as system gain (SG, see Section 3.5 of Chapter 3).

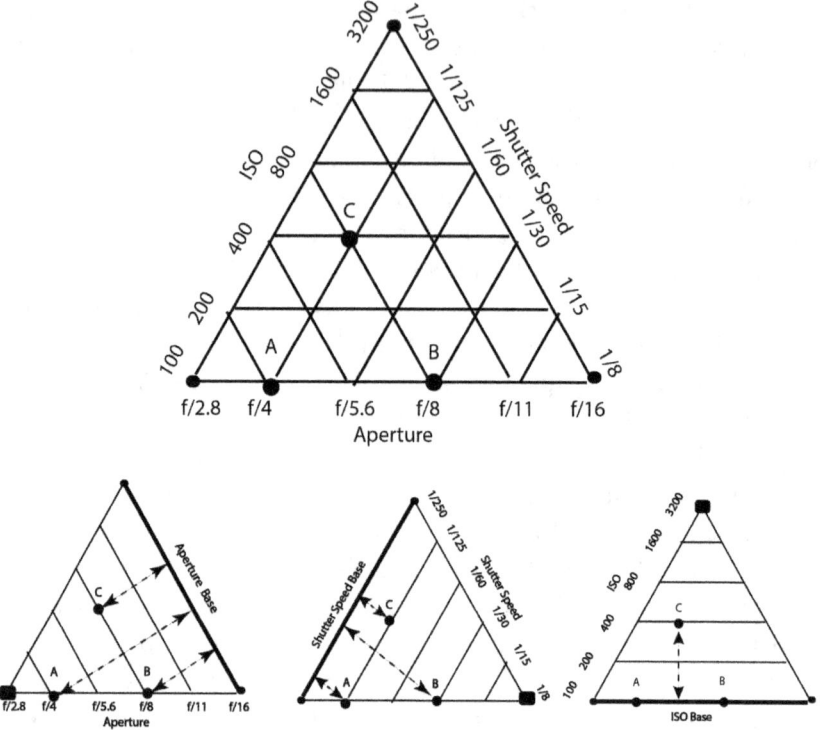

Fig. 7.1. (Top) Exposure triangle that is conveniently used to describe how different combinations of aperture $(f/\#)$, time of exposure or shutter speed, and ISO setting can produce the same photographic exposure. The triangle consists of the three overlapping grids shown in the lower portion and explained in the text.

The next step is to understand the advantages or disadvantages of equivalent exposures corresponding to different points in the exposure triangle.

7.1.1 *Aperture Effects*

The aperture images shown in Fig. 7.2 illustrate the vanes that turn to open or close the diameter D_{aper} of the nearly circular regions for typical values of $f/\#$. As mentioned above, the f number $(f/\#)$ is defined as the ratio of D_{aper} to the true focal length of the lens.

Table 7.2. Values of $f/\#$, Δt, and ISO and the corresponding brightness selection.

	$(f/\#)^2$	Δt	ISO	BS
A	$(1/4)^2$	$(1/125)$	100	0.05
B	$(1/8)^2$	$(1/30)$	100	0.05
C	$(1/8)^2$	$(1/125)$	400	0.05

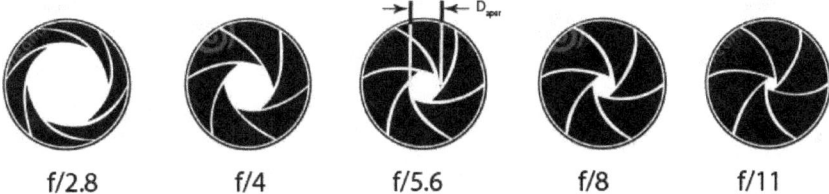

f/2.8   f/4   f/5.6   f/8   f/11

Fig. 7.2. Schematic illustration of five of the camera apertures listed in Fig. 7.1. The aperture control on the camera pivots each of the vanes so as to adjust the open area. The open area can be approximated by a circle of diameter D_{aper}. Although successive changes in diameter or $f/\#$ vary in steps with ratios that are approximately equal to the square root of $\sqrt{2} \approx 1.4$, such that the corresponding open areas vary in steps of 2.

Thus, for an $f/16$ camera setting, the diameter is the small value of $D_{\mathrm{aper}} = f/16$. Typical relative aperture areas corresponding to the tick marks $fn = f/16, f/11, f/8, f/5.6, f/4, f/2.8$, etc., increase in ratios near to $\sqrt{2}$ of the corresponding aperture areas, or relative brightness varying by ratios near to 2.

The other important image feature that is affected by the aperture size is known as *depth of focus*. This is particularly important for portrait photography, where one often wants the background image behind the facial features to be blurred in order to not distract from the portrait itself. The effect arises from the fact that the distance from lens to focus varies with the distance from camera to object, see Eqs. (2.3) and/or (2.7). The ray tracing sections for the region near the focus are shown in Fig. 7.3 for three different object distances D_O from the lens. Rays (a) that are in focus come together at the entrance to one pixel a distance D_I from the aperture.[4] Rays (b) that are slightly out of focus would come together slightly behind the CMOS pixel; however, since all these rays strike the same pixel as the rays (a), this object is perceived as being *in focus*. In contrast, rays (c) only come together a distance δD_I behind the CMOS pixel. Since some of these rays only strike the neighbors of the central pixel, the image of the object that produced rays (c) is blurred. The issue to address is how large a difference in object distances will cause a blurred image.

The primary effect of aperture size on the depth of focus is to set the angle β in Fig. 7.3 that defines the angular range of the image-forming rays. It should be obvious that $\beta \sim D_{\text{aperture}}/D_I$, and for large object distances, where $D_I \sim f$, one has the approximation $\beta \sim D_{\text{aperture}}/f$. In this approximation, $\beta \sim f/\#$. Using this

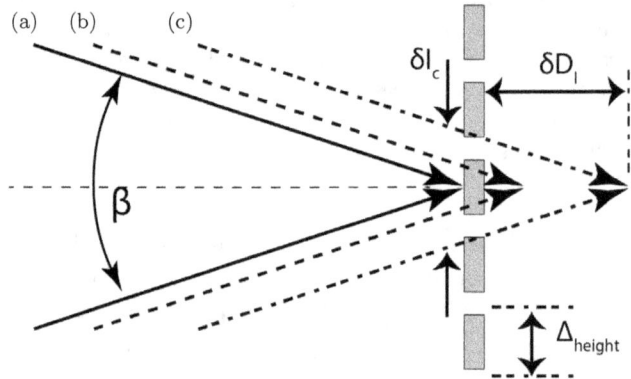

Fig. 7.3. Portion of a ray diagram near the focal point of a lens for three images of objects at the focus (a), near the focus but still focused (b), and focused behind the CMOS plane by a distance δD_I. Ray (c) is not focused. This illustration is applicable to the hypothetical monochromatic camera that was discussed in Section 3.3.

---

[4] As was discussed in Section 3.3 of Chapter 3, the same simplifying assumption of a monochromatic sensor is used here. In reality, the conditions for the focusing of rays involve all three red, green, and blue pixels, and when color is considered, the quantity Δ_{height} should be replaced by a variable that is typically two times larger.

approximation, the size of the spread in the rays (c) at the CMOS would be approximately $\delta I_c \sim (\delta D_I)\,(f/\#)$. On the other hand, for the rays (b), the pixel height is larger than the width of the light spread, and with $\Delta_{\text{height}} \geq (\delta D_I)(f/\#)$, all of the rays (b) would be intercepted by the pixel. For all intents and purposes, these rays could be considered to be in focus. Thus, the range of object distances that can be considered to be in focus are those for which the image distance is[5]

$$\delta D_I < \Delta_{\text{height}}/(f/\#). \tag{7.2}$$

Referring back to Eq. (2.3), it can be shown that the distance δD_I caused by two objects a distance δD_O apart satisfy

$$0 = \frac{1}{D_O - \delta D_O} - \frac{1}{D_O} + \frac{1}{D_I - \delta D_I} - \frac{1}{D_I}.$$

When $D_O \gg f_{\text{true}}$, the value of δD_O can be approximated as

$$\delta D_O \approx -D_O^2 \frac{\delta D_I}{f_{\text{true}}^2}. \tag{7.3}$$

Taking $\delta D_I = \Delta_{\text{height}}/(f/\#)$, the absolute value of the depth of focus is given by

$$|\delta D_O| \approx \frac{D_0^2}{f_{\text{true}}^2}\left(\frac{\Delta_{\text{height}}}{f/\#}\right)^2 = \left(\frac{D_O}{f/\#}\right)^2\left(\frac{\Delta_{\text{height}}}{f_{\text{true}}}\right)^2. \tag{7.4}$$

The most important lesson from this expression is that smaller depths of focus are produced with larger apertures. To put it another way, an $f/2$ aperture produces a depth of focus that is $(2/16)^2$ smaller than an $f/16$ aperture. As an aside, note that the tiny aperture in the pinhole camera shown in Fig. 2.1 has an unlimited depth of focus.

7.1.2 *Shutter Speed Effects and Image Stabilization*

The types of shutters that control the exposure time Δt are discussed in Section 7.4. For now, we only deal with the effects that Δt have on exposure. It is obvious that photographs of rapidly moving objects,

---

[5]See footnote 4 explaining the reason why Δ_{height} should be replaced by a value that is about twice as large when color is taken into account.

such as in sports events and other moving events, require suitably short Δt exposure times; however, there are two other circumstances for which shorter Δt are called for. The first of these are scenes with extremely bright light, such as a very sunny beach or a bright snow-covered scene. For any such scene, a normal Δt, such as 1/60 of a second, along with an $f/16$ and ISO of 100 could induce a stored electron number in excess of the full well capacity of a single pixel. In this situation, it is hard to avoid overexposure without shortening Δt. This is sort of obvious and doesn't really need further discussion. On the other hand, there is one other situation that does warrant some explanation.

For most people, an exposure with a hand-held camera is nearly always accompanied by some degree of *camera shake* that can cause image blurring. The general rule of thumb for avoiding this effect is to shoot the image at a shooting speed $\Delta t < 1/f_{\mathrm{equiv}}$.[6] On the other hand, virtually all modern consumer cameras have built-in *image stabilization* mechanisms that reduce camera shake, making it possible to shoot with Δt that can vary from two to twenty times longer, depending on the camera.

Of course, there are other ways to implement shorter Δt. My own favorite when walking is to carry a monopod. These are light and relatively small, and some of them double as *walking sticks*. Tripods are the standard that is most often employed with long focal length lenses. On the other hand, simply holding the camera against an adjacent wall is a good expedient when nothing else is available. The one thing to avoid is holding the camera, or smart phone, at arm's length in order to view the screen on the back of the camera. This is a frequent cause of some measurable image blurring.

7.1.3 *ISO Setting Effects*

The third element that makes up the exposure triangle is the ISO scale that controls the system gain (SG), which was defined by Eq. (3.8) in Section 3.5. The most common nominal ISO value of

---

[6]https://en.wikipedia.org/wiki/Image_stabilization.

100 usually corresponds to an SG = 25. This setting has the effect that something like 100,000 stored photoelectrons in the CMOS well will be converted by the ADU processor to a digital value of the order of $100,000/25 = 4,000 \sim 2^{12}$. In Section 3.5 of Chapter 3 and Section 4.7 of Chapter 4, we have already pointed out that this number is considerably larger than the 8-bit range (2^8) of virtually all commercial computer displays. One lesson to be drawn from this observation is that perfectly adequate images can be formed with fewer photoelectrons. This is what happens when larger *ISO* settings are chosen. The effect is to produce comparable digital values for fewer photoelectrons. This is a tool for rendering acceptable images with lower illuminations.

The sketch in Fig. 7.4 illustrates the manner in which the three lowest ISO values convert different numbers of stored electrons in a pixel to the same ADU value. Taking the black bar at ISO = 100 to represent the number of electrons corresponding to the *full well capacity* of one pixel, the sketch illustrates that half the number of electrons at ISO = 200 will result in the same ADU value as for the full well capacity at ISO = 100. The next bar illustrates that the same ADU value would be produced for a number of electrons that is only one-quarter of the full well capacity if the ISO is 2^2 larger, i.e. ISO = 400 = 100×2^2. This is the explanation by which the third leg of the *exposure triangle* can be invoked to produce satisfactory

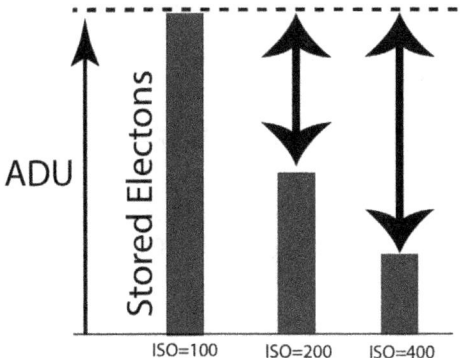

Fig. 7.4. Illustration showing how ISO steps of 2^n result in the same ADU values for numbers of stored electrons that are $1/2^n$ times smaller.

exposures in low-light conditions. Unfortunately, as was the case for the other two legs, the exposure adjustment is accompanied by an undesirable side effect.

For any exposure, the photons, and therefore the photoelectrons, are added to the CMOS well at some average rate of $\dot{n}$ (electrons/second) such that for a long enough time δt, the recorded number would be $n = \dot{n}\delta t$; however, if δt is short or $\dot{n}$ is small, the actual number in any one exposure can turn out to be either slightly larger or smaller than n. That is, the actual number recorded at some time δt can be $n(\delta t) = \dot{n}\delta t + \delta n$, where the value of δn or an individual exposure can span a range of values that are given by a probability distribution known as Poisson's law.[7] The principal prediction from Poisson's law is that the mean square value of the variance is given by

$$\langle \delta n^2 \rangle = n = \dot{n}\delta t. \tag{7.5}$$

It follows that for large ISO values, for which the number of stored electrons is small, the apparent exposure of neighboring pixels that might normally have identical exposures can vary by $\sqrt{\langle \delta n^2 \rangle}$. In particular, the relative variations in the exposure δBS are given by

$$\delta\text{BS} \approx \frac{\sqrt{\dot{n}\delta t}}{\dot{n}\delta t} = \frac{1}{\sqrt{n}}, \tag{7.6}$$

implying that, for small numbers of stored electrons, there would be larger variations, or speckles, in the intensity of adjacent pixels that are identically exposed. An example of this effect is shown in Fig. 7.5.

7.2 Optical vs. Digital Zoom

The two zoom features of a camera both expand the area being photographed; however, they do it in two different ways. Optical zoom adjusts the physical optics to reduce the field of view in order to magnify a small section of the image. The way this is done is that it increases f_{true} (and also f_{equiv}) in order to reduce the angle subtended by the area being photographed. This has the effect of magnifying the details in the image. Using the notation introduced earlier,

---

[7]https://en.wikipedia.org/wiki/Poisson_distribution.

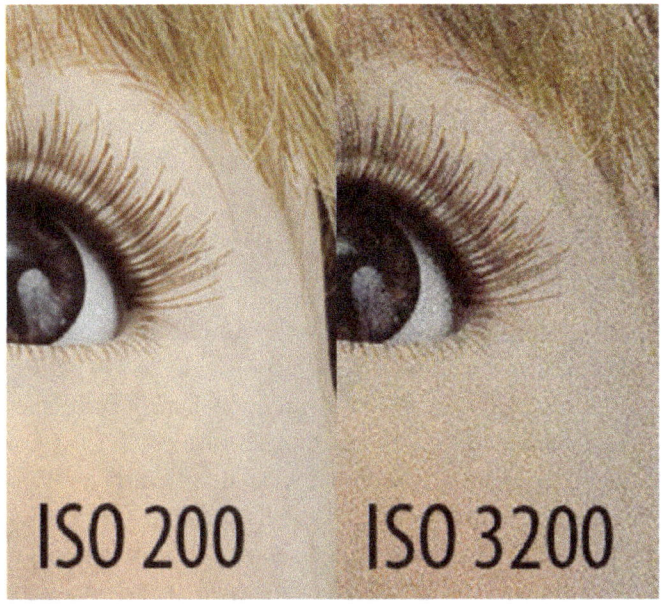

Fig. 7.5. Illustration of the appearance of speckles in an exposure taken at large ISO.[8]

the pre-zoomed minimum-resolved image detail, which is the original source-resolution $\Delta_{\text{source-rew}}$, is coarser than the minimum-resolved detail, or $\Delta_{\text{source-res}}$, in the zoomed image. To put this another way, the image is magnified, so the same number of pixels are utilized to store a smaller part of the scene.

In contrast, digital zoom simply selects and magnifies a small section of the image stored in the original, or un-zoomed, image. Even though the optics isn't changed, this has the effect of producing a larger, or magnified, image. Unfortunately, although the image is larger, the number of resolved details is unchanged. The effect is that a given size in the magnified image has fewer resolved details. To put this another way, while digital zoom can produce a final image of the same size as optical zoom, any given region of the image will have less detail than the optically zoomed image. In fact, the only reason

---

[8]https://photographylife.com/what-is-iso-in-photography.

for invoking digital zoom while taking a photograph is to increase the size of the image in the onboard image viewer on the camera display. The exact same level of magnification can be achieved by editing an image after it is transferred to a computer. Whether done on the computer or by digital zoom on the camera, the resulting image is grainier than the optically zoomed image.

7.2.1 *Perspective*

Another effect that accompanies both optical and digital zooming that the photographer should be aware of is referred to as *perspective*. The principal method by which we judge the size of objects that we photograph is their size in relation to other objects in the photograph. For example, Fig. 7.6(a) is a schematic illustration of the relative height of two images (to the right) of the red and green bars (on the left). The fact that the green image is large than the red is caused by the fact that the red bar is further from the lens. In contrast, Fig. 7.6(b) illustrates the images of the two objects when they are moved together further away from the lens. Note that the two are the same height and the same distance apart in both (a) and (b);

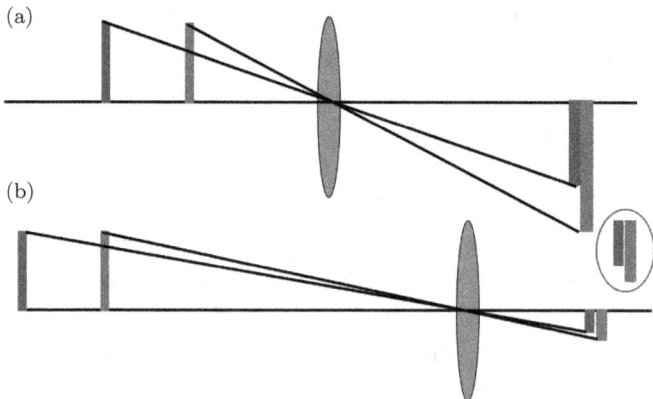

Fig. 7.6. Diagram illustrating the *perspective effect*, in which the relative height of objects being photographed changes with distance from the camera. To make this more visible the inset displays an enlarged version of the image in (b).

however, the relative heights of the red and green images in (b) are closer to each of those in (b) than in (a). The obvious reason for this is that as they move further from the lens, the angles that they subtend become closer. The effect would be even stronger if they were even further from the lens.

The important point to make here is that although news photographs often exhibit this effect in images taken using telescopic lenses with long focal lengths, the effect is only due to the distance between object and camera and not the focal length, whose only purpose is to make the image larger. The very same perspective effect would appear in images taken with shorter focal length lenses and later magnified in the computer to produce images that are the same height as the one taken with a telephoto lens. Of course, the same effect occurs for images produced by electronic zoom. This is particularly important in portrait photography, where the object is relatively close to the camera. In general, portrait images taken with a subject much closer than 100 mm will exhibit detectable facial effects due to perspective distortions.

7.3 Aliasing

One effect that appears with digital photography that film cameras did not encounter is known as *aliasing*, sometimes referred to as *moiré*. The problem occurs when photographing something like a brick wall or a picket fence that has a periodic, repeating pattern. It is hard to avoid a situation in which the periodic pattern of the CMOS sensor and that of the image on the sensor get out of step.

Figure 7.7 illustrates the effect of the overlap of two periodic patterns with slightly different repeat structures. A single structure is shown in (a). Part (b) magnifies three different portions of the two slightly different waves. On the left, one can see that the peaks of both waves more or less coincide; in the middle, one can see that the peaks of the upper wave coincide with the troughs of the lower. Finally, further along, the peaks more or less coincide again. Part (c) displays the moiré pattern of the overlap of the two waves.

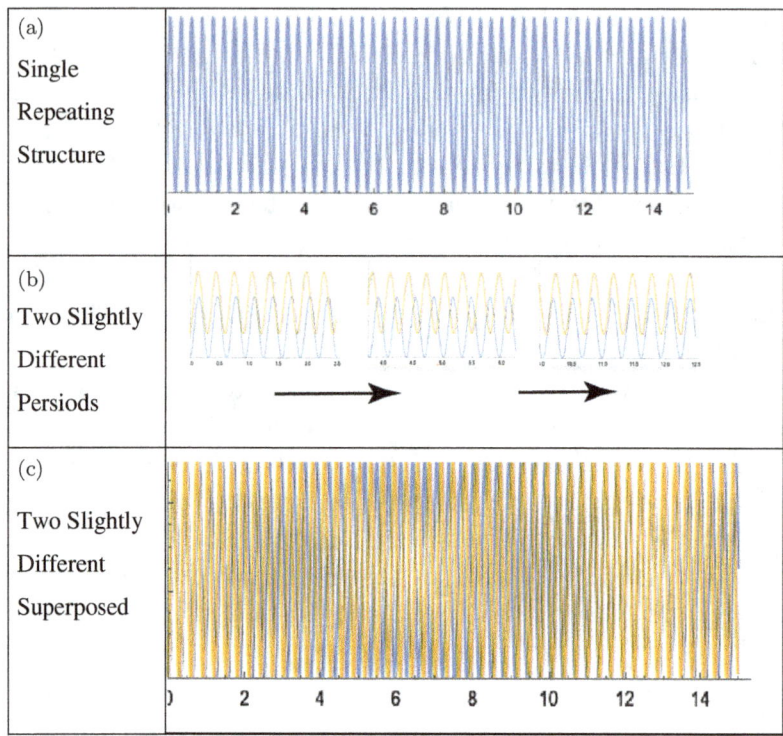

Fig. 7.7. Example of two repeating waves with slightly different periods: (a) Illustration of one wave; (b) displaced sections of two waves with slightly different repeat periods; (c) superposition illustrating moiré pattern for structures in (b).

A photographic example of the moiré effect is shown in Fig. 7.8. On the left, camera processing, which is described in the following, is used to eliminate the moiré effect that is evident on the right. Although some high-end cameras can be treated to remove what is known as an *antialiasing filter*, this cannot be done for the majority of consumer cameras. My guess is that camera manufacturers were concerned that consumers would be unhappy with the moiré effect and elected to insert a smearing filter that would average out the short-distance pixel structures in the processed image. With this filter in place, the camera processor does not display the periodic structure of the CMOS that is shown in Fig. 3.5

Brick wall sampled to avoid aliasing   Brick wall sampled with aliasing

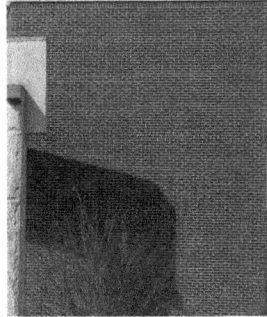   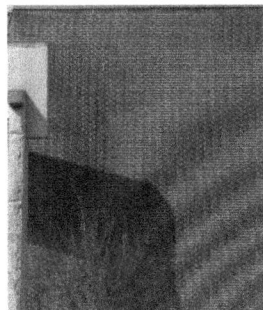

Fig. 7.8. Example of the moiré effect in a photograph. On the left, the camera was treated to eliminate the effect that is visible on the right.

The unfortunate price paid for this is that the image resolution is smeared out to be broader than the results described in Section 3.3 of Chapter 3.

7.4 Shutters

The shutter situation for digital cameras is somewhat complicated in that there are both mechanical and electronic shutters and that they each have different versions with different advantages and disadvantages. Things were considerably simpler in the days of film cameras, when there were primarily only two types of mechanical shutters. On the other hand, the best digital cameras typically have both mechanical and electronic shutters, along with software that allows them to take advantage of the best properties of both. The problem is that the camera manufacturers do not usually list the types of shutters for their cameras. In the following, we describe the two types of mechanical and electronic shutters that are in common use. Unfortunately, users will have to search to learn the particular shutter types of specific cameras.

The upper portion of Fig. 7.9 shows an example from the user manual for the Sony RX10 camera. This camera gives the user the option of using either a mechanical or electronic shutter; however, nowhere in the documentation is the type of mechanical or electronic

Sony RX10

⌼ Shutter Type	Sets whether a mechanical shutter or an electronic shutter is used when shooting still images.

Excerpts from Nikon Spec Sheets

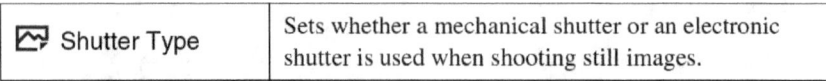

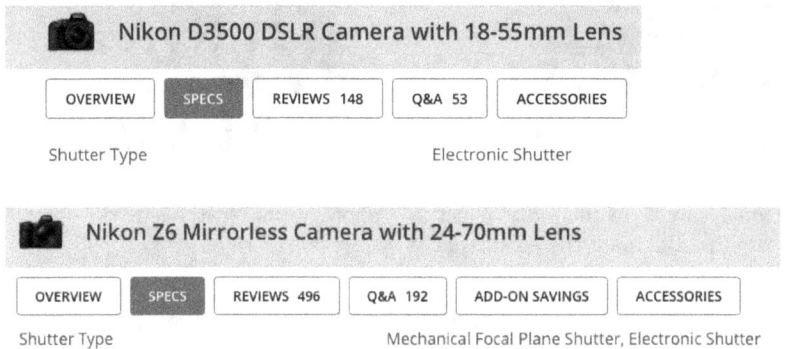

Fig. 7.9. Examples of the documentation showing the shutter specs for three typical consumer cameras.

shutter described. The two lower portions of Fig. 7.9 display excerpts from the specification sheets for two Nikon cameras. The D3500 specifies an electronic shutter but not the type. The specification for the Nikon Z6 does mention the type of mechanical shutter but not the type of electronic shutter.

7.4.1 *Mechanical Shutters*

The *focal plane shutter* is the most common mechanical shutter. This is the one used in all but the high-end digital cameras. It consists of an opaque screen immediately in front of the CMOS sensor that moves through the focused image in times that can be as fast as the order of 1/10,000 of a second. An illustrative sketch of the shutter screen motion is shown in Fig. 7.10. On activation, the lower screen moves down, uncovering more and more of the sensor (1). After the time set by the shutter speed, the upper screen moves down (2) to completely cover the sensor. Each section of the sensor is only uncovered for a time Δt. One disadvantage of this type of shutter

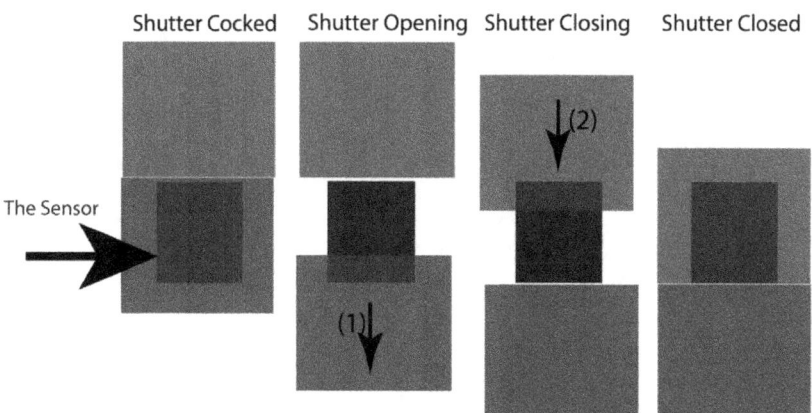

Fig. 7.10. Illustration of the screen motions for the two screens of a focal plane shutter. Prior to the shutter opening, the two screens completely cover the sensor. On activation, the lower screen moves down, uncovering more and more of the sensor (1). After the set shutter time governed by Δt, the upper screen moves down (2) to completely cover the sensor. Each section of the sensor is only uncovered for a time Δt.

is that since the exposed time at different parts of the image occurs at slightly different times, this type of shutter can distort rapidly moving images. The shortest values of Δt for this type of shutter are on the order of 1/2000 to 1/10,000 of a second. Another disadvantage of this focal plane shutter is that since the different parts of the image are exposed at different times, it isn't really practical to synchronize the exposure with a camera flash.

The alternative mechanical shutter is known as the *leaf shutter*. Typically, this shutter is installed within or very near the lens. It is typically constructed from moveable leaves, such as those in the aperture shown in Fig. 7.11. The image to the left shows the closed position of the leaves when the shutter is cocked before opening. Once opened, the leaves move to the position in the center figure, and after Δt, they close again. The advantage of this location is that since every portion of the lens produces the same full image, different parts of the image are exposed for the same time interval of Δt. Typically, the shortest open times for a leaf shutter are on the order of 1/500 of a second.

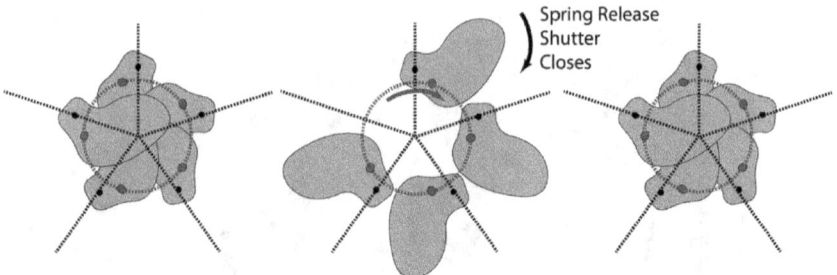

Fig. 7.11. Schematic illustration of the leaves' motion in opening a leaf shutter. Typically, these types of shutters have more than the four leaves drawn here.

The unfortunate plight of the leaf shutter is that, to be most effective in uniformly exposing the image, it works best when it is built into the lens. This has the effect of making leaf shutters for external lenses more expensive. Consequently, although Leica and other high-end cameras often have external lenses with leaf shutters, they are mostly only used in cameras with fixed lenses. On the other hand, flash synchronization with this type of shutter is straightforward.

The principal disadvantage of either type of mechanical shutter is that, like all mechanical devices with moving parts, they are susceptible to wear and damage. A second feature that some users do not like is the noise that they make on closing. Finally, the mechanical motion tends to induce some degree of camera shake. It is also worth noting that the manufacture of cameras with moving parts does add cost in comparison to cameras that only have electronic shutters, as discussed in the following.

7.4.2 *Electronic Shutters*

The two principal types of electronic shutters are known as *rolling* and *global*. The global is the simplest to describe since it can simply be thought of as a *snapshot* shutter. Prior to exposure, it drains all of the electrons from every pixel in the CMOS sensor. Following that, it turns on every pixel so that they all accumulate charge simultaneously. When the exposure is over, the charges are drained and converted to ADU units, as discussed in Secton 3.5 Flash synchronization with global shutters is straightforward. These shutters can also be relatively fast, with Δt less than 10 μs.

In a reflection of their name, rolling shutters operate by sequentially exposing individual rows in the CMOS one at a time. Consequently, in a way that is similar to the focal plane mechanical shutter, each line in the image is exposed at slightly different times. Typically, it takes about 10 μs to expose each row, and the total time to record one snapshot with a 3000-line CMOS sensor is of the order of $3000 \times 10\mu s = 30\,ms$. This seems rather slow, but these systems actually download the stored data in each row simultaneously with the exposures of the preceding rows. This means that exposures are a continuous process such that videos and other similar recordings can be done with virtually no dead time. Furthermore, if one is photographing a slowly moving scene such that the time delay for different rows is not considerable, the exposure time to be employed with the exposure triangle is the time per row, which, as mentioned above, can be only of the order of 10 μs. The principal shortcoming of the rolling shutter is that flash synchronization is not feasible.

7.5 Focus

Virtually every digital camera has a variety of *focus areas* that the user can select for manual focusing or autofocusing. One selection of these from the SONY website is shown in Table 7.3. Each camera manufacturer has an equivalent set of selections that are best described in either the camera user manual or the manufacturer's website. The ability of virtually all digital cameras to focus automatically is one of the great advantages of the modern digital camera. In the following, we describe the two primary *passive focusing systems* in digital cameras. In addition to the passive systems described here, some cameras also use an *active focusing system* that makes use of the echo from either an ultrasonic or infrared light wave emitted from the camera to measure the distance to the object. The principal advantage of the active systems is that they do not rely on ambient light and can be used with flash illumination in the dark.

Table 7.3. Typical selectable camera focus areas.

Focal Area	Focusing Property
Wide	Focuses across the entire monitor
Zone	Focuses on the area within the zone selected on the monitor, and often has multiple focus areas
Center Fix	Focuses on subjects centered in the monitor
Spot	Focus on small objects, or narrow areas

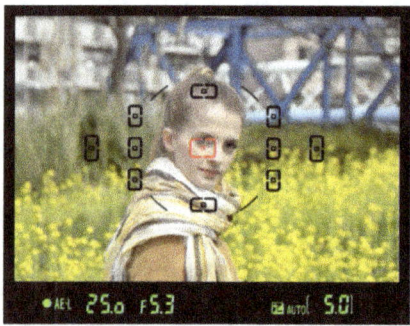 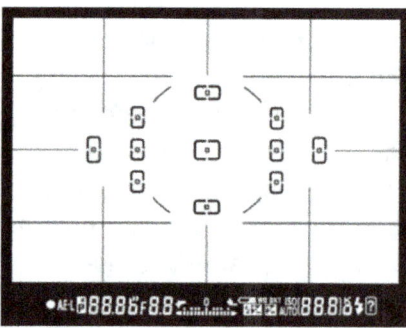

Fig. 7.12. (Left) Sample Nikon viewfinder screen showing the focal points that can be used for autofocusing. (Right) The same focal points without the superposed image.
Source: https://imaging.nikon.com/lineup/dslr/basics/16/02.htm.

Another feature is that most cameras have some number of autofocus (AF) points that facilitate the different focus areas. Typically, these vary in the order of 10–50 points distributed over the face of the sensor. One example of these that is shown in Fig. 7.12 is copied from the Nikon website.

7.5.1 *Automatic Focusing Methods*

7.5.1.1 *Phase detection*

The phase detection method for *autofocusing* is illustrated in Fig. 7.13. The panel on the left shows the light rays that form an out-of-focus image a distance δD_I past the main sensor (MS) plane. The "unfocused" image in the right panel shows light rays that are focused

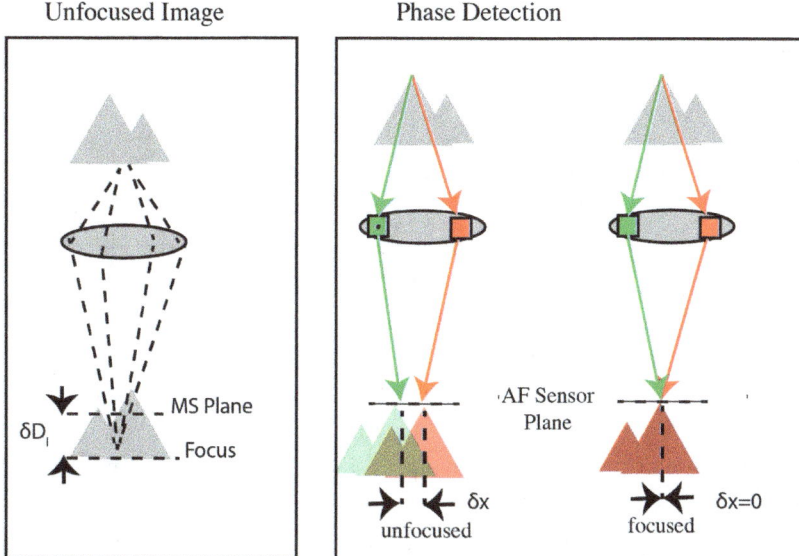

Fig. 7.13. Illustration of the phase detection method for autofocusing: The left panel illustrates an example in which the image is focused a distance δD_I past the focal plane of the main sensor. The right panel illustrates the positions of the images in a second sensor referred to as the *phase detection sensor*. These images are formed by small secondary lenses at the side of the main lens. The displaced position of these two images δx is proportional to δD_I. The camera software measures δx and uses the information to refocus the main image to bring δD_i and δx to zero, as illustrated in the focused figure.

on the separate *phase detection* sensor (AF sensor plane) through two subsidiary optics at the side of the main lens. The *phase detection* sensor is different from the main sensor. As indicated, the red and green images from these two apertures in the unfocused image focus in the *phase detection sensor* are at positions a distance δx apart. The optics is designed such that $\delta x \propto \delta D_I$. The camera software interprets δx and uses the measured value to adjust the lens so that δD_I is moved to zero. When this is done, the image is in focus on the MS plane.

One advantage of this type of focus, in contrast to the contrast detection discussed in the following, is that it only requires a single measurement of δx to bring the image into focus. This makes the process rather rapid and allows image tracking for moving objects.

7.5.1.2 *Contrast detection*

The second common method of autofocusing, known as *contrast detection*, is somewhat simpler. Typically, the camera software will evaluate the intensity differences in adjacent pixels in one row, or column, in the CMOS array. The scene is determined to be *out of focus* so long as the intensity in adjacent pixels is more or less the same. The camera software keeps searching for the focus in order to minimize these intensity differences. An example of the out-of-focus and in-focus samples are illustrated in Fig. 7.14. The optimum focus is determined when the contrast between adjacent pixels is maximized.

Contrast detection is more accurate than phase autocontrast in that it analyzes most points in the sensor; however, the price paid for the accuracy is that it is slower. The reason is that the phase method requires only one measurement from which the lens adjustment that is needed to focus can be calculated. In contrast, as mentioned above, the search procedure used by the contrast method is essentially slower. A second disadvantage of the contrast method is that, for lower-priced cameras, the features that are used for contrast are usually vertical edges. The implication of this is that focusing may depend on the orientation of the camera.

 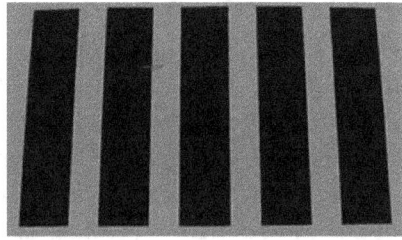

Fig. 7.14. Illustration of out-of-focus and in-focus samples from a pixel strip. *Source*: https://electronics.howstuffworks.com/autofocus.htm.

Chapter 8

Technical Addendum

8.1 Radians, Solid Angles, and Small Angle Approximation

The degree is probably the most common unit by which angles are expressed. The full circle has $360°$, and right angles, which are $1/4$ of this, have $90°$. In this book, as well as for many applications in physics and engineering, the radian is an alternative measure of angles. The angle θ, as shown in Fig. 8.1, corresponding to about $25°$, subtends the arc ab on the circle of radius $R = 1$. The radian value of θ is defined to be equal to the length of ab divided by the radius (value $= 1$). Thus, the full circle of $360°$ corresponds to 2π radians (i.e. the circumference of a circle is $2\pi \times$ radius), and a right angle of $90°$ corresponds to $1/4$ of the full circle, or $\pi/2$ radians. Most of the optics discussed in this book make use of what is known as *small angle approximation*, which is usually applicable when θ is smaller than about $6°$. For example, when $\theta = 6°$, the value in radians is $2\pi(6°/360°) = 0.1047$. For small angles, the value of θ in radians is roughly equal to the value of the usual trigonometric functions $\sin(\theta) = bc/ob = 0.1045$ and $\tan(\theta) = bc/oc = 0.1051$. The differences between θ and these functions become even smaller for smaller values of θ. Thus, when invoking the *small angle approximation*, one can make the approximation that $\sin(\theta) = \tan(\theta) = \theta$. Referring to Fig. 8.1, for small angles with $R = 1$, the value of $\theta \approx ba \approx bc$.

111

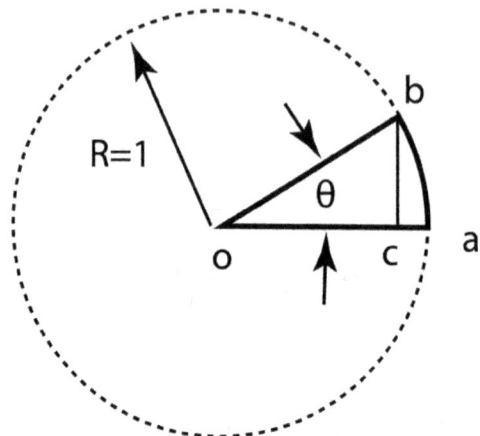

Fig. 8.1. Schematic illustration of angle notations.

In a similar way, a *solid angle* is defined as the area of a section of a sphere A_{sph} divided by the square of the sphere radius, i.e. $\Omega = A_{\text{sph}}/R^2$. Since the area of a sphere is $4\pi R^2$, the full solid angle subtended by a sphere is $\Omega = 4\pi$.

8.2 Binary Numbers

Digital computers process data through arrays of binary switches that can be either on or off. For example, if a switch is off, it is assigned the value 0, while for the on position, the values of different switches are defined to be numbers like $1, 2, 4, 8, \ldots, 2^n$, where n varies in steps of 1 from 0 to some set maximum. The actual data are constructed through a combination of these switches. For example, an 8-bit number would have eight switches that have the values $S_1 = (0 \text{ or } 1), S_2 = (0 \text{ or } 2), S_4 = (0 \text{ or } 4), S_8 = (0 \text{ or } 8), \ldots, S_{128} = (0 \text{ or } 128)$ (i.e. $128 = 2^7$). On the other hand, when expressed as a binary number, the order of the switches runs from high to low $\{S_{128}, S_{64}, S_{32}, S_{16}, S_8, S_4, S_2, S_1\}$ such that the binary representation of a number like 149, which is equal to $128 + 16 + 4 + 1$, would have only S_{128}, S_{16}, S_4, and S_1 turned on and all the others turned off. The binary representation is thus (10010101). The largest 8-bit number with all switches on corresponds to $128+64+32+16+8+4+2+1 = 255 = 2^8 - 1$. Similarly, the largest 14-bit number has a value of $2^{14} - 1 = 16383$. Binary fractions are similar; however, in place of the switch values of $(1, 2, 4, \ldots)$ they refer to $(1/2, 1/4, 1/8, \ldots)$. Thus, in binary, the decimal value of $1.625 = 1 + 0.5 + 0 + 0.125$ is 1.101.

In view of the fact that the *bit* numbering system becomes somewhat unwieldy for numbers much larger than $2^8 = 256$, this is the value by which the byte is defined. In this way such that one *byte* corresponds to 8 bits. Thus, the 4-bit ($2^4 = 16$) is only 1/2 byte and the 8-bit *RGB* standard is only 1 byte. The 16-bit system becomes $2^{16} = 65{,}546 = 2$ bytes. The advantage becomes more apparent for larger numbers like 1 Kilobyte $= 1{,}024$ bytes, which is $8 \times 1024 = 8{,}192$ bits, one Megabyte $= (1024)^2 = 1{,}048{,}576$ bytes, or 8,388,608 bits, and one Gigabyte $= (1024)^3 = 1{,}073{,}741{,}824$ bytes. This is often simplified by saying that a Kilobyte (KB) is about a thousand bytes, a Megabyte (MB) is about a million bytes, a Gigabyte (GB) is about a billion bytes, etc.

8.2.1 *File Size of RAW Image*

With the above, one can estimate the bit size of an image. The method of estimating the size of a RAW image, $\text{Size}_{\text{Raw-bits}}$, can be illustrated by considering the image created by a camera, such as the Nikon D780, as listed in Table 3.2. This camera has a sensor with $N_{\text{pix}} = 25$ Megapixels, and for a 12-bit image, the size of a RAW image is

$$\text{Size}_{\text{Raw}} = (10^6 \times N_{\text{pix}})N_{\text{bit-depth}} = (10^6 \times 25) \times 12 = 300 \times 10^6 \text{ bits.}$$
$$(8.1)$$

To convert to MB, this number must be divided by 8 bits/byte and again by $(1024)^2$ to convert bytes to MB.

$$\text{Size}_{\text{Raw-MB}} = (10^6 \times N_{\text{pix}})N_{\text{bit-depth}}/(8 \times 1024^2)$$
$$= (300 \times 10^6)/(8 \times 1024^2) \cong 36 \text{ MB.} \qquad (8.2)$$

To put this in a condensed form, the size of a RAW file can be written as

$$\text{Size}_{\text{Raw-MB}} = (N_{\text{pix}})N_{\text{bit-depth}}/(8.389). \qquad (8.3)$$

The calculation is illustrated in Table 8.1.

Table 8.1. Illustration of the file size calculation in Eq. (8.3).

Variables		Values
Number of Pixels	Megapixels	25
Bit Depth	Bits	12
Size of Raw Image	Megabytes	$25 \times 12/8.389 = 35.76$

8.3 Geometry of Exposure Triangle

The geometry that serves the basis for the *exposure triangle*, as illustrated in Fig. 7.1, can be understood with the help of Fig. 8.2.

The area of the equilateral triangle in Fig. 8.2 is $(H \times L)/2$. The areas of the three enclosed smaller triangles A, B, and C are similarly $(a \times L)/2, (b \times L)/2$, and $(c \times L)/2$, respectively. Obviously, the sum of these three areas are equal to the area of the larger triangle,

$$(H \times L)/2 = (a \times L)/2 + (b \times L)/2 + (c \times L)/2 = (a + b + c) \times L/2,$$

implying that $H = a + b + c$ regardless of where the point P is located.

The application of this geometry to the exposure triangle can be seen by recognizing that the shutter speed, aperture, and ISO scales in Fig. 7.1 are defined in steps of 2^n. For example, the shutter speed

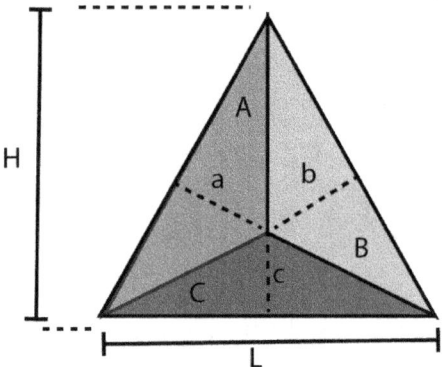

Fig. 8.2. Diagram illustrating the geometry that serves the basis of the exposure triangle introduced in Section 7.1 of Chapter 7 (Fig. 7.1).

Table 8.2. Values of nA, nS, and nI for the corresponding brightness selections shown in Fig. 7.1 and Table 7.2. The equality of BS_{binary} for the three exposures is another demonstration of the validity of the exposure triangle.

	nA	nS	nI	BS_{binary}
A	4	1	0	5
B	2	3	0	5
C	2	1	2	5

scale can be expressed as follows: Shutter speed $= (1/256) \times 2^{nS}$, where nS varies from 0 to 5.[1] Since the size of the aperture is given by the square of the $f/\#$, the scale for aperture $= (f/16)^2 \times 2^{nA}$, where nA, like nS, varies from 0 to 5. Similarly, the values for the ISO scale are given by ISO $= 100 \times (2^{nI})$. With this notation, the binary brightness can be expressed as

$$BS_{binary} = nA + nS + nI, \tag{8.4}$$

as an alternative to Eq. (7.1). Defined this way, the values of the lengths of the perpendiculars for the examples in Fig. 7.1 that are given in Table 8.2, along with the values for BS_{binary}, are a very direct demonstration of the validity of the exposure triangle.

---

[1]Camera manufacturers typically round off to values of $1/256 \sim 1/250$.

www.ingramcontent.com/pod-product-compliance
Lightning Source LLC
Chambersburg PA
CBHW071513220526
45472CB00003B/1012